# Wales

# Wales

Text by Richard Keen
Photography by Ian Burgum

Weidenfeld & Nicolson
London

# INTRODUCTION

## Snowdon – Yr Wyddfa

*Tremendous Snowdon! while I
    gradual climb
Thy craggy heights, through
    intermingled clouds
Various of watery grey, and
    fable hue
Obscure the uncertain prospect,
    from thy brow
His wildest views the mountain
    genius flings*

Wrote W Southey in a sonnet composed after his tour through Wales in 1794. Yr Wyddfa is the highest peak of the Snowdon massif – the remnant of ancient, weathered volcanoes. The mountain has a special significance to the people of Wales, representing the very heart of an area that has retained its essential Welshness.

There are many ways to reach the top, 1,085m (3,560 ft) above sea level. Take the easy way and ride the well-engineered rack railway, opened in 1896, drawn by steam locomotives, but there are more energetic alternatives up the alpine-like paths and scree slopes. For the lucky ones, the clouds may part to reveal some of the most outstanding views in Britain. Close to Llyn Llydaw, on the slopes of Snowdon, is a cave where sleeps King Arthur and his followers awaiting the clarion call to deliver the country from a terrible, but unspecified, fate.

Two main factors have fashioned the landscape of Wales – geology and climate. Some of the oldest rocks, dating from the late Precambrian period, are to be found alongside the Menai Straits and at St David's Head. Many places bear marks of the last Ice Age, ending a mere 10,000 years ago, when ice flows scoured out hollows and sliced the sides of mountains. Wales has a complex geology with rocks of various types and origins visible across the land. A number of geological terms in worldwide use originate in this country. Ordovician and Silurian refer to two tribes in Wales, the Ordovices and the Silures, and Cambrian is derived from the Roman word for Wales.

In the face of prevailing westerly winds, climate and topography have influenced the patterns of settlement and ways of life for thousands of years. Below the surface of the land, exploitable deposits formed during geological upheavals were another influence on the shape of the land and the growth of its communities. The rock of the North West has been worked for centuries to produce roofing materials, creating a network of small towns and villages overshadowed by steep mountains. Exploitation of coal measures in South Wales produced a way of life that was as vibrant as it was harsh.

At the core of Wales are its mountains – the sharp, rugged peaks of the North and the soft, rolling hills of the South. Around the core are the coastal plains and border lands. The division in the way of life between the upland and lowland areas was often clear. A tourist in 1746, John Torbuck, commented that the 'Country is mountainous, and yields handsome clambering for Goats, and hath a variety of Precipice to break one's neck; which a man may sooner do than fill his Belly, the Soil being barren and an excellent place to breed a famine in'. Yet Daniel Defoe found the area around Carmarthen when he visited in 1724 'Abounds in corn, and in fine flourishing meadows, as good as most are in Britain, and in which are fed, a very great number of good cattle'. There is hardly a place in Wales where evidence of human occupation cannot be found. Even some of the wide, open moorlands were created by felling trees and over grazing. Elsewhere, evidence may be less visible, sometimes a grassed mound or merely a crop mark. The cities and towns tell their own stories in the layout of their streets and their architecture.

Areas such as Snowdonia or the Pembrokeshire coastline are well known. Other parts are, too, but perhaps carry different images in the minds of visitors – the view of the great

# NORTH WEST

## Harlech Castle and North Wales

The view of Harlech Castle standing above the long sweep of coastline and against a spectacular backdrop of the mountains is one of the most enduring images you can take away of Wales.

Concepts of the land have changed considerably since the time the castle was in use and the hinterland was crossed by few trackways and the mountain areas were described as 'barren and uncharitable'. It was the 18th- and 19th-century travellers in search of romantic and picturesque experiences who helped change the way we view the land. The castle stands solid and permanent, but the views change constantly as sunlight and shadow throw the mountains into sharp relief or cloud the image and give a sense of mystery – and sometimes foreboding.

The rugged skyline of Snowdonia is a relic of ancient volcanic activity. The rocks that form its backbone are composed of lava and volcanic debris that were mixed with deposits on the floor of the Ordovician sea. This makes it possible to find fossilized sea shells in the shales that form the very summit of Snowdon. The igneous peaks that include Carneddau, Moel Siabod, Moel Hebog and Cader Idris have, by their extreme hardness, resisted erosion and now stand in sharp relief against the surrounding land.

The sedimentary rocks that form the beds of slate are composed of layer upon layer of fine-grained mud that has been subjected to great pressure and heat. The resulting strata have planes of cleavage that are not coincidental with the original bedding planes, enabling them to be easily split into blocks and sheets. Where the deposits of workable rock lay close to the surface quarries were opened, and the communities around Nantlle, Corris, Ffestiniog, Bethesda and Llanberis developed.

Early slate quarries were little more than mere scratchings supplying local markets, but towards the middle of the 18th century a larger market began to develop as towns expanded in Britain and elsewhere. The industry grew in the 19th century to reach peak production in 1898, when almost half a million tons of slate were produced. Slate was exported worldwide but the main markets lay in Europe and very close links developed between Porthmadog and Hamburg. The transportation of slate from quarries to ports was expensive and slow until narrow-gauge railways began to appear. Today, the Ffestiniog Railway is best known because, instead of slate, it carries passengers between Porthmadog and Blaenau Ffestiniog. Until steam power was introduced in 1863, the trucks were hauled by horses. The line climbs steadily from sea level into the mountains, so on the downward journey the horses rode in a special 'dandy wagon'. There are just a few quarries still at work today supplying a small but steady demand, and a number of workings have been opened as visitor attractions.

The geology of the area has been traced back 570 million years, with Precambrian deposits lying either side of the Menai Straits and reaching down into Llŷn. The Ice Age that ended about 10,000 years ago produced some of the most spectacular effects. Nant Ffrancon and the Llanberis Pass are good examples of the characteristic U-shaped valleys formed by the movement of ice flows.

## Source of the Severn

The Pumlumon range of hills rises to a peak of nearly 760m (2,500ft) and forms a physical barrier between northern and southern Wales. There is debate about the derivation of the name. It could come from 'lluman' meaning a banner, or 'llumon', a beacon. In the watershed of these hills rises the River Severn, of which Drayton wrote:

*And for the second place, proud
    Severn doth strive,
Fetch her descent from Wales,
    from that proud mountain
    sprung,
Plynillimon, whose praises
    frequent them among,
As of that princely maid, whose
    name she boasts to bear,
Bright Sabrine, whom she holds
    as her undoubted heir.*

This river begins as a series of small, dark pools draining a peaty bog. George Borrow described the source as a 'little pool of water some twenty inches long, six wide, and about three deep. It is covered at the bottom with small stones, from between which the water gushes up.' Within a few miles of the source, another great river, the Wye, begins its journey from the uplands, eventually disgorging into the Severn near Chepstow.

## Tŷ Mawr
### Nr Penmachno

Tŷ Mawr, literally 'large house', was the birthplace, in 1541, of William Morgan, later to become Bishop Morgan, the son of a humble copyholder. Bishop Morgan, the translator of the Bible into Welsh, a task he completed in 1588, has an important place in the history of Wales.

Queen Elizabeth I was conscious of the division that had formed between the anglicized landowners and middling classes and the ordinary people of Wales. Realizing that the 'gwerin' – the majority of the people – were deprived of religious contact in their native tongue, she issued an Act ordering the translation of the Bible into Welsh. The Act's preamble stated that English 'is not understood by the greatest number of her majesty's most loving and obedient subjects inhabiting the country of Wales, who therefore are utterly destituted of God's Holy word, and do remain in the like or more darkness and ignorance than they were in the time of papistry.'

The style of language used by Bishop Morgan was based on that of the great Welsh poets but was not pedantic. The use of Welsh in the churches gave status and credibility to the language.

## Dolgellau

Dolgellau has grown out of its surrounding mountains and still bears witness to the observation made by Richard Fenton in 1808 that: 'Masonry at Dogelly merits particular notice. From time immemorial they have built with very large stones, even to the top, lifting the Stones to the work from towards the middle course with an immense machine which takes above a day to erect, and worked by two men, every stone being of such weight as to require a Lever of that vast power.'

Dolgellau was the main market town of Merioneth and a principal centre of the wool trade. By 1838, eight water-powered mills provided employment for 50 hands. As early as 1775, a traveller had described Dolgellau and its industry as 'no despicable town for these parts'. In the 18th century, the town supported Y Gymdeithas Loerig (The Lunar Society), which met at every full moon to discuss literary matters. William Thackeray stayed in the town and wrote in the visitors' book of his hotel:

*If ever you come to Dolgelly,*
*Don't stay at the . . . Hotel,*
*For there's nothing to put in*
*   your belly*
*And no one to answer your bell.*

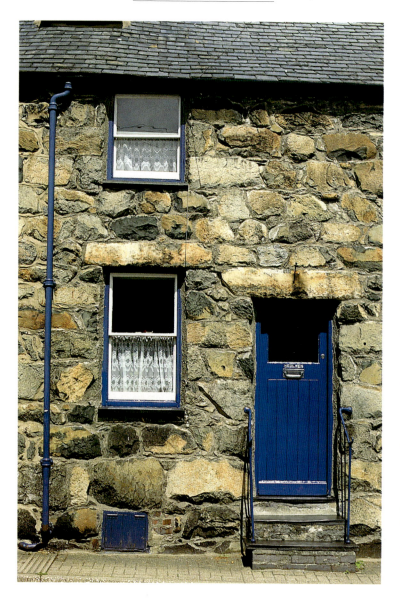

## Castell y Bere
### *Nr Abergondwyn*

Brut y Tywysogyon (Chronicle of the Princes) refers to 1240 as the 'year of Christ when Llywelyn ap Iorwerth, prince of Wales, a man whose deeds were difficult to relate, died'. The end of the 12th and the early years of the 13th centuries in Wales was a time of internecine strife and constant pressure from across the border. Llywelyn, son of Iorwerth, united the princes of independent Wales and, by his political and military skill, achieved a period of peace – even to the extent of gathering the quarrelling princes together to form a national parliament.

He built Castell y Bere in the Dysynni valley on a promontory of rock that overlooked one of the main lines of communication during the Middle Ages. The castle was taken by Edward I in 1283, but 11 years later it was attacked by Madog ap Llywelyn, together with its small borough, and burned. After that, the castle disappeared into historical obscurity and now only its ruins, still with some very fine decoration to see, are testimony to its former importance. In the valley, at the foot of Cadair Idris, is Craig y Deryn, the rock of birds.

## The Roman Steps
*Nr Llanbedr*

The paved trackway that climbs the slopes of Rhinog Fawr, known as the Roman Steps, is the route of a pathway built at the end of the 13th century to serve Edward I's castle at Harlech. It supplemented seaborne supply lines and, until the introduction of modern road systems, it continued in use as a packhorse trail.

The pathway climbs through sparse woodland, across bogs and past huge rocks and boulders to break the ridge on the northern slope of Rhinog Fawr. Below lies Coed-y-Brenin, to the north is the reflection of light from the water of Llyn Trawsfynydd, and beyond are the quarried hills surrounding Blaenau Ffestiniog. On the Ordinance Survey map, a well is marked near the top of the path, which must have been most welcome for the travellers climbing its steep slope.

Rhinog Fawr and Rhinog Fach dominate the main ridge of mountains above Harlech, which were formed by the massive uplift of the underlying Cambrian beds. The erosion-resistant thick beds of grit have left the rugged landscape of the twin peaks broken by the pass of Bwlch Drws Ardudwy to the south.

## Penmon
*Nr Beaumaris*

The dovecote at Penmon dates from approximately 1600 and was probably built by Sir Richard Bulkeley, the local landowner. Inside there are nesting boxes for about 1,000 birds and the remains of a stone pillar that supported a ladder giving access to the nests. The roof is expertly corbelled to the stone lantern to allow access for the birds.

Penmon is a holy place probably founded in the 6th century by St Seiriol. The presence of a spring of good water was essential for baptisms and healing. Near the holy well is a simple hut of stone thought to be St Seiriol's cell.

The church was burned by invading Danes and then rebuilt between 1120 and 1170. In 1237, Llywelyn ap Iorwerth gave the church to the monks of Priestholm, a small, holy island on the east coast of Anglesey. They moved to Penmon, built the monastic range of buildings and reorganized themselves as Augustine Canons. In 1810 an antiquarian, Richard Fenton, thought it to be 'the most perfect specimen of an old Saxon pile of the most monastick kind now extant in Wales'. Nearby is a very fine carved stone cross, which was probably erected around the year 1000 to replace an earlier one destroyed in a Viking raid.

### Tre'r Ceiri

The antiquary Thomas Pennant made the steep ascent to the top of Yr Eifl on Llŷn in 1781 and saw 'the most perfect and magnificent, as well as the most artful, of any British post I ever beheld'. Tre'r Ceiri is the largest stone-walled hill fort in Britain. The continuous stone wall is in places 4m (13ft) high, and the main entrance is constructed to funnel incomers into a narrow gap, overlooked on all sides. Inside are the remains of approximately 150 circular, oval and rectangular buildings.

The fort dates from the Iron Age, although archaeological finds indicate that the site was in use during the Roman occupation. From the summit there is a striking view across Yr Eifl and along the Llŷn peninsula.

Thomas Pennant was accompanied on his tours through North Wales by Moses Griffiths, whose drawings of many of the sites visited were described by Pennant as: 'the performance of a worthy servant whom I keep for that purpose. The candid will excuse any little imperfections they may find in them; as they are the works of an untaught genius, drawn from the most remote and obscure parts of North Wales.'

### Dyfi Furnace,
*Furnace*

The Dyfi iron furnace, in the village of Furnace, was founded in 1755 by Vernon, Kendall & Co, a family of ironmasters from the West Midlands of England. Iron was produced for about 50 years using charcoal that was produced in great quantities in the neighbouring woods. To raise the temperature high enough to smelt iron ore, a waterwheel drove large bellows that blasted air into the base of the furnace. The Dyfi furnace originally supplied pig iron to local forges. When iron making ceased, the buildings were converted into a sawmill that produced pit props for the coal mining industry. The present waterwheel draws its water from the head of a delightful waterfall.

A manuscript in the National Library of Wales states the 'pigs of Dyfi furnace are smelted with charcoal and therefore preferable to . . . others reduced with coak fire'. When furnaces were tapped, the molten iron was guided into a central trough in the casting floor. From the main trough, smaller side channels were opened at right angles. Early ironmasters saw a similarity between this layout and a sow feeding her piglets – hence the terms 'pig' and 'sow' iron.

## Glaslyn Estuary

The *North Wales Gazette* reported in July 1811 the completion of an embankment at the mouth of River Glaslyn: 'To attempt to enter into the merits of the individual gentleman who has finished this great work, amidst difficulties incalculable to the common mind, we feel ourselves inadequate to the task.'

It was part of an ambitious land-reclamation scheme undertaken by William Alexander Madocks, owner of a local estate and an energetic improver possessed of great dreams and ambitions. Among his successful schemes was the reclamation of 3,000 acres of land at Traeth Mawr and the Glaslyn estuary. He also envisaged the provision of a short cut to Ireland via the natural harbour of Porth Dinllaen on Llŷn. The road connection to Porth Dinllaen never materialized but the construction of the embankment, or the Cob as it is known locally, proved to be of great importance. The engineering required the diversion of the river and this in turn scoured out the sea approaches, allowing ocean going craft access to the shore. With the opening of the Ffestiniog railway linking with Blaenau Ffestiniog across the Cob on 20 April 1836, the slate port of Porthmadog developed rapidly.

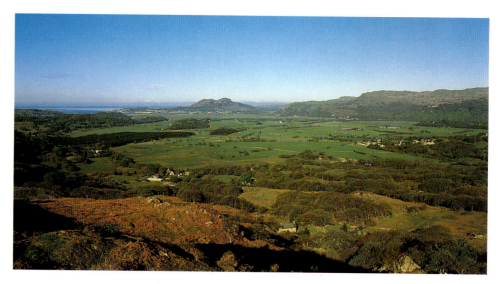

## Porth Dinllaen
*Nr Nefyn*

Because of its sheltered location and easy access from western shipping lanes, Porth Dinllaen was seriously considered as the main packet station for Ireland. Some local landowners and entrepreneurs were involved in building and improving road access, including William Madocks whose model town of Tremadog was designed with access to Porth Dinllaen in mind.

Its main competitor was Holyhead, and the decision by Parliament in 1819 that the main route from Shrewsbury should cross the Menai Straits into Anglesey ended all hopes. But the supporters of Porth Dinllaen were not dismayed and, later in the century, petitioned that the new railway system should be directed across Wales. Instead, the coastal route was chosen, and the Stephensons' tubular bridges at Conwy and across the Menai Straits ensured Holyhead's success. Porth Dinllaen remains a small, peaceful fishing community that has changed little over the years. It has recently been acquired by the National Trust and its character will remain largely unaltered.

## Dolbadarn Castle and Llanberis Pass

J M W Turner exhibited his painting of Dolbadarn Castle, North Wales at the Royal Academy in 1802. He had visited Llanberis in 1798 and 1799 and produced a number of colour sketches. The castle, against the backdrop of Llanberis Pass, made a perfect study for him. All the elements were there for an artist much taken with the sublime and the power of nature.

The castle was built by Llywelyn ap Iorwerth, probably in about 1230. His grandson, Llywelyn the Last, was imprisoned in the castle for 20 years by his brother, Owain Goch, until 1277. Turner was moved to write a poem to accompany his painting.

*How awful is the silence of the waste.*
*Where nature lifts her mountains to the sky.*
*Majestic solitude, behold the tower*
*Where hopeless OWEN, long imprison'd pin'd*
*And wrung his hands for liberty, in vain.*

Beyond, the road climbs sharply up the narrow glaciated pass littered with boulders deposited by ice flows.

## Dinas Oleu
*Nr Barmouth*

Dinas Oleu, the Fortress of Light, has a special place in the history of conservation in Britain – it was the first property to be acquired by the fledgling National Trust in 1895.

One of the founders of the National Trust, Canon Hardwicke Rawnsley, was staying with his friend Mrs Fanny Talbot in Barmouth when he received the Articles of Association for the new organization. Mrs Talbot immediately offered a small area of land overlooking the broad sweep of the bay to the Trust, writing: 'Your National Trust will be of the greatest use to me. I have long wanted to secure for the public forever the enjoyment of Dinas Oleu, but I wish to put it into the custody of some society that will never vulgarise it, or prevent wild Nature from having its own way.'

From the top of the rocky outcrop the views range across Cardigan Bay towards the Llŷn peninsula and Bardsey Island, and then southwards across the broad estuary.

Octavia Hill, another founder member of the Trust, upon learning of its acquisition, mused: 'We've acquired our first property; I wonder if it will be our last?'

## Port Penrhyn
*Nr Bangor*

The narrow-gauge railways of North Wales were crucial to the expansion of the slate industry, linking the often remote quarries to the coast.

Lord Penrhyn expanded the quarries at Penrhyn to become the largest in the world in the 19th century, and created a slate-exporting harbour called Port Penrhyn. His one-time agent was Benjamin Wyatt, who designed the late-Georgian port office.

Prior to the opening of the horse-drawn railway in 1801, moving slate from quarry to port involved 400 road wagons and 140 men, although the quarry was only 9.5km (6 miles) from Port Penrhyn. The railway transformed the quarry, and enabled the port to develop rapidly. Workshops were opened to service the port, along with a slate-sawing shed, producing fire surrounds and gravestones, and a factory making writing slates and pencils.

The needs of the workforce were catered for in the circular, conically roofed building, housing a number of lavatories. Provision of slate partitions has provided space for generations of graffiti artists for their initials, names and drawings of ships and locomotives.

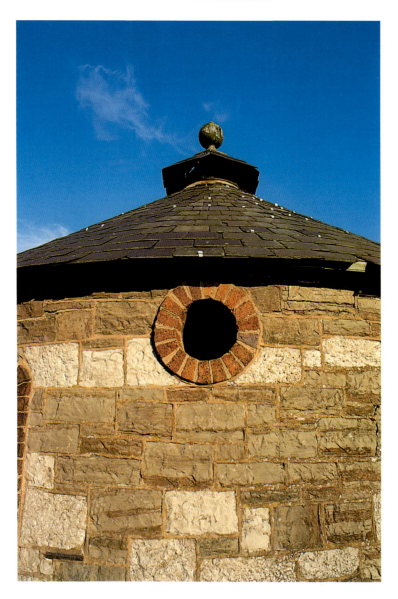

## Llanddwyn Island
*Anglesey*

The western seaboard is still a busy sea lane and the coast of Wales has had the dubious distinction of being fraught with dangers for seafarers.

From the 18th century onwards, increased traffic required effective lighthouses. An Act of 1836 enabled Trinity House to buy all the privately owned lights and to embark on a programme of improvement and renewal.

Llanddwyn Island faces southwards towards the approaches to the Menai Straits. From the 1830s it became the base for Caernarfon pilots, who brought ocean-going craft safely through treacherously shifting sandbanks into Caernarfon and Port Dinorwig. It was common practice to erect white-washed navigation markers at prominent points. The one at Llanddwyn Island probably dates from the early years of the 19th century and was originally unlit. The first coastal light was illuminated on 1 January 1846 at the base of a tower that was similar in design to the windmills on Anglesey.

## Parys Copper Mine
*Anglesey*

The sheer size of the 'greatest copper mine in the World' is astonishing. During the 18th century, massive quantities of low-grade copper ore lying relatively close to the surface were exploited on a large scale. Huge open-cast pits were dug and shafts sunk to reach the lower deposits.

From the mid 18th century the twin mines of Parys and Mona became the most important copper mines in Britain, supplying the smelters at nearby Amlwch and exporting to Swansea and St Helens.

The ore was separated from the rock by beating it with hammers, a task usually undertaken by the copar ledis (copper ladies). For a 12-hour shift they were paid 10 pence. Protection for their hands was provided by leather gloves with iron rings around the fingers. Employing children from the age of eight was considered by the company to be a form of charity.

Dr John Rutty recommended to the Royal Society in 1760 that the water pumped from the workings had excellent healing properties and could cure a multitude of ailments, including 'ulcers, the itch, mange, scab, dysenteries and haemorrhages'.

## Cwm Idwal

Charles Darwin visited Cwm Idwal in 1831 seeking evidence of glaciation. He wrote: 'We spent many hours in Cwm Idwal, examining all the rocks with extreme care . . . but neither of us [he was accompanied by Professor Adam Sedgwick] saw a trace of the wonderful glacial phenomena all around us.' When he visited again 10 years later he recognized his omission and stated that evidence of glaciation was 'so conspicuous that a house burned down did not tell its fate more plainly than did this valley'.

The steeply eroded slopes tumble downwards into a dark lake. Boulders scattered around were deposited by the same ice flows that formed the lateral and terminal moraines.

The presence of rare alpine flora was one of the reasons that Cwm Idwal was designated a nature reserve in 1954. Much of the research on the local plant life was carried out by Evan Roberts, a quarryman from Capel Curig. He was entirely self-taught and his detailed observations resulted in his being awarded an honorary MSc by University College of Wales, Aberystwyth in 1956. In the last few years of his life he lost his sight, but he was still able to identify plant species by their scent and texture.

## Penrhyn Castle
*Nr Bangor*

In 1820, G H Dawkins Pennant commissioned Thomas Hopper to build what today is acknowledged as one of the most magnificent examples of Norman Revivalist architecture.

The family owned the huge and successful Penrhyn slate quarries at Bethesda and throughout the house slate has been used in many ways – as building blocks, flooring and even a massive state bed, which weighs more than a ton. Queen Victoria visited Penrhyn in 1859 and slept in a state bed made of oak, designed by Thomas Hopper.

Much of the furniture and contents of the house are original, ranging from paintings by Canaletto and Richard Wilson to a collection of steam engines and railway memorabilia. The drawing room is opulent, with silk hangings and carved woodwork. This was very much the domain of the ladies of the house. When guests were being entertained it was not unusual for them to change their outfits five or six times in a day.

The house offers many fine vistas. One of these is of Anglesey and another is of the Great Orme, while the Snowdon massif rises to the south.

## Plas Newydd
*Anglesey*

Late in the afternoon of 18 June 1815 the Earl of Uxbridge said to the Duke of Wellington: 'By God, sir, I've lost my leg.' To which the Duke replied: 'By God, sir, so you have.' The unfortunate Earl's leg was shattered by grapeshot at the Battle of Waterloo, during which he had performed outstandingly well. He survived his wound and, on returning home, was made 1st Marquess of Anglesey.

The Marquess was provided with an articulated artificial leg, the design of which proved so successful that it was still being produced in 1914. One of these legs, along with clothing and equipment used at the Battle of Waterloo, is now on display in the family home of Plas Newydd.

The house overlooks the Menai Straits and dates from about 1470, but its appearance today is the result of changes and additions made between 1783-86 and 1793-99.

The 6th Marquess commissioned Rex Whistler to paint a mural in the dining room of imaginary scenes and familiar landmarks, including the Round Tower at Windsor Castle. The artist can be seen sweeping leaves – the last self-portrait before his death in action during World War II.

## Cwm Croesor
*Nr Penrhyndeudraeth*

The official opening on 1 August 1864 of the Rhosydd Slate Quarry narrow-gauge incline and railway down Cwm Croesor gave a direct link into the port of Porthmadog. The incline is 213m (700ft) long and descends sharply over a horizontal distance of 396m (1,300ft). It was operated by gravity and the descending, fully laden trucks hauled up the empties. On the floor of the valley it joins with a neighbouring quarry incline.

Some of the quarrymen lived during the week in damp, flea-ridden, overcrowded barracks with poor sanitary conditions; others walked up to 8km (5 miles) to and from work each day.

Cwm Croesor is a classic example of a glaciated valley. As recently as 10,000 years ago, North Wales was covered by ice that in places could have been 275m (900ft) thick. Many of the glaciers were of such size that their movement produced the characteristic U-shaped, steep-sided valleys.

The workmen in the quarry formed a choir and on summer evenings walked out to the head of the incline and sang to the valley below.

## Bardsey Island

Ynys Enlli – Bardsey Island – was named after a Viking, Bardr, and is reputed to be the burial place of more than 20,000 saints. A Celtic *clas* was founded in the 6th century, one of many island sanctuaries of the period.

Giraldus Cambrensis, who was born c. 1146 and accompanied Archbishop Baldwin through Wales preaching for the Third Crusade, thought the island had special qualities. 'This island, either from the wholesomeness of its climate, owing to its vicinity to Ireland, or rather from some miracle obtained by the merits of the saints, has this wonderful peculiarity, that the oldest people die first, because diseases are uncommon and scarcely any die except from extreme old age.'

An Augustine monastery was established in the 12th century, considered to be one of the most important in Wales. With the dissolution of the monasteries the buildings were abandoned, and a survey of 1538 reported that 'no land has ever been cultivated because of the ravages of rabbits with which this land is plentifully supplied'. It was reputed that during the 19th century so numerous were the human bones discovered there that they were used to make fences.

## Harlech Castle

Harlech Castle speaks of dominance and strength. Built between 1283 and 1289, it was an important link in the chain of castles established by Edward I. The building work was overseen by a master mason, James of St George, whose skills are apparent in many of the castles of North Wales. In recognition of his work he was awarded a pension in 1284 of three shillings a day for life. In 1290, he was appointed Constable of Harlech Castle. Remarkably, the castle still looks much as it did when it was completed, with many of the walls and towers at approximately their finished height.

Despite its position and strength, the castle was taken by Owain Glyn Dŵr in 1404, and for the next five years it was his court and family home. *The Gossiping Guide to Wales*, published in 1895, refers to an event in its history when, during the Wars of the Roses, the fortress was under siege: '. . . and according to a bard of that age there was very bloody work, for he recounts the slaughter in figures that would make a Colenso dubious indeed, slaying 6,000 men at the entrance gates.' The siege features in the repertoire of most male voice choirs when they sing 'Men of Harlech'.

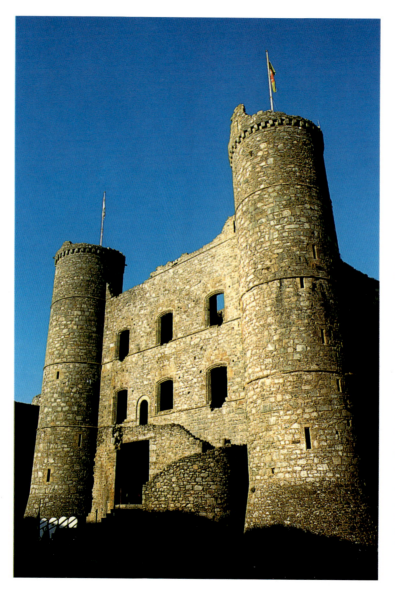

## South Stack Lighthouse
*Holy Island, Anglesey*

George Borrow paid his guide half a crown to show him Pen Caer Gybi, more familiarly known as Holyhead Mountain. 'Shaping our course westward we came to the vicinity of a lighthouse, standing on the verge of a precipice, the foot of which was washed by the sea.' South Stack Lighthouse was built in 1808 by David Alexander, who also designed Dartmoor Prison. The building materials were lowered by a cable way, later used to supply the lighthouse, and was replaced by a bridge in 1828. The lighthouse, which serves the shipping lanes for Holyhead Harbour, was automated in 1984.

At the western extremity of Anglesey, Holy Island is an important archaeological landscape with evidence of occupation stretching back to the late neolithic period. The Holyhead Mountain hut group consists of about 50 buildings. Carbon dating has placed the complex as late neolithic or early Bronze Age. They are known as Cytiau'r Gwyddelod (the Irishmen's Huts), the name being indicative of the importance of the relationship between Ireland and the western seaboard of Wales.

## Portmeirion

The architectural imagination of Sir Clough Williams Ellis reached great heights with the creation of this Italianate village overlooking the Glaslyn estuary. To build the village, he collected architectural items from far and wide, between 1926 and his death in 1978.

A neo-classical colonnade from Bristol and a Gothic *porte-cochere* from Clwyd were among the pieces incorporated in his scheme. Plaques and figures adorn the buildings and every corner turned reveals another delight – a fountain enclosed in a courtyard or a view glimpsed through an archway. Traffic is not allowed in the narrow streets that climb from the Portmeirion Hotel.

Many notable writers have visited the village, including G B Shaw, H G Wells and Daphne du Maurier. While staying at Portmeirion, Noel Coward wrote *Blithe Spirit*. The village was also used as the location for the 1960s television series 'The Prisoner', which still attracts something of a cult following. The village is surrounded by gardens and woodland and is fronted by a long, sandy beach.

With so many imported elements, Portmeirion should be out of place in its environment. But it is a tribute to the genius of the architect that Italy should sit so comfortably in Wales.

## Workhouse at Minffordd
*Nr Penryhndeuraeth*

A gloomy corridor forms the spine of the building. Leading off is a series of small narrow cells, each with its prison-like door complete with spy hole. An iron bed fixed by chains to the wall virtually fills the cell and at the end of the confined space a door gives access into a room, about 1m (3ft) square. It is illuminated by a small window opening, closed by an iron plate into which a series of circular apertures is let.

This was the Casual Ward of the Minffordd Workhouse where, in return for food and accommodation, inmates would find the floors of their small cells covered with large stones that they would have to break into pieces small enough to pass through the apertures. The broken stone was then used by the overseers for the repair of local toll roads. The workhouse is complete with a fumigation chamber, where inmates' clothes were cleaned, and separate washing facilities for men and women.

A report of 1834 stated: 'Our intention is to make the workhouses as like prisons as possible and to establish therein a discipline so severe and repulsive as to make them a terror to the poor and prevent them from entering.'

## Gilfach Ddu, Llanberis

*It has truly been said, as we all
    must deplore
That Grenville and Pitt have
    made peers by the score;
But now 'tis asserted, unless I
    have blundered.
There's a man that makes peer-
    esses here by the hundred . . .*

The extract is from a 19th-century
poem written by a circuit judge
who was amused by the names
given to the different sizes of
slate. Among the smallest were
'ladies', while some of the largest
were known as 'queens', with
variations that included 'narrow
ladies' and 'large queens'.

One of the most productive
quarries was the Dinorwig
Quarry at Llanberis. Over 4,500
men and boys were employed
there in the late 19th century. To
maintain all the essential machinery and equipment, the company
built workshops at Gilfach Ddu,
on the northern shore of Llŷn
Padarn, in 1870. The buildings
and machines have been preserved by the National Museum
of Wales. Power to drive the
machines came initially from an
enormous waterwheel 15m (50ft)
in diameter. All the needs of the
quarry could be met by the
workshops, whose interiors have
hardly changed – except for the
addition of a few displays.

## Dylife
### Nr Machynlleth

North west of Llanidloes on the
mountain road to Machynlleth
at Dylife (place of floods) is a
spectacular example of erosion.
At the head of the Twymyn
Valley the river changes course
abruptly to cascade over a waterfall. It originally ran in an entirely
different direction at a higher
level but was 'captured' when
glaciation in the lower valley
eroded the sides sufficiently to
cause the upper river to change
course. Over the millennia the
river has continued to deepen the
valley, creating the characteristic
V-shape formation.

Nearby is the community of
Staylittle – appropriately named
since it was a stopping place for
coaches that ventured into the
remote uplands. A Roman fortlet
called Pen-y-Crocbren, (gibbet
hill) is close by. A set of gibbeting
irons dating from c. 1700 were
found in a mound above the
fort in 1938, together with a
human skull.

The Star Inn at Dylife once
served the small community of
lead miners and their families.
The remains of their houses and
chapels are now, however, little
more than crumbling walls and
mounds of stone.

## Menai Suspension Bridge

A number of schemes were put forward to bridge the Menai Straits but none met the conditions imposed by the Admiralty that there should not be any 'impediments in the movement of ships'.

It was Thomas Telford who overcame the restrictions with a masterpiece of engineering that set new standards in bridge design. The first chain was slung into position in April 1825 and to celebrate three workmen ran its swaying length. All four chains were in position by the following July and the Menai Town Band gave a performance from a platform mounted in the middle.

The bridge was opened in January 1826 and the resident engineer W A Provis wrote that on the first day 'the bridge was so crowded that it was difficult to move along. Most of the carriages of the neighbouring gentry, stage coaches, Post Chaises, gigs and horses passed repeatedly over and kept up a procession for several hours. The demand for tickets was so great that they could not be issued fast enough and many in the madness of their joy threw their tickets away that they might have the pleasure of paying again.'

## Beaumaris Court House

Beau Marais derives from the Norman French fair marsh and grew around the last of Edward I's castles, which was started in 1295. The town follows the classic grid pattern and the streets are still narrow and crowded. The architecture is mainly 19th century with exceptionally fine houses looking across the Menai Straits towards Snowdonia.

Careful examination reveals older buildings sometimes hidden behind very ordinary exteriors. The court house holds many surprises, and on stepping through its doors an instant transition is made to 1614 when it was built. Until 1971 it was the oldest building in Britain where an assize court was still held. In the 19th century, railings were erected to keep the public area separate from the actual court and a special box is set aside for 'The Mayor and Bailiffs of the Borough of Beaumaris'.

The sentences meted out could be harsh. In 1773, Mary Hughes was sentenced to be transported for seven years for stealing clothes valued at 11 pence. Many persons brought before the bench found themselves serving sentences in Beaumaris jail, which is preserved and, like the court house, is open to the public.

### St Cybi's Well
*Nr Pwllheli*

The Llŷn peninsula reaches towards the saintly island of Bardsey and is dotted with churches, holy wells and springs. Saints were perceived as ordinary mortals who, through their special qualities, were elevated to become intermediaries between God and men. They were often healers and many were associated with wells where sufferers could find ease. The holy well dedicated to the 6th-century Saint Cybi is hidden in a small valley covered in sessile oaks and highlighted with bright yellow flowering gorse bushes.

Water still rises from the well set in a small, roofless building of large, rough-hewn stone blocks. Adjoining the well are the remains of a small 18th-century cottage, the home of an old lady who supplemented her income with the tips she received from visitors seeking help. A paved pathway leads towards a privy, a short distance downstream so as not to pollute the holy water. Richard Fenton, antiquary and barrister, visited the well on Saturday, 7 August 1813 and wrote that the well 'has been much resorted to for complaints in the limbs and the eyes, but the faith in such sainted wells is daily diminishing'.

### Blaenau Ffestiniog

The poet Guto'r Glyn wrote an ode in the 15th century to Richard Kyffin, Dean of Bangor:

*I intend to raise a house on the hill a fair residence is this hall if we have tiles and wooden nails I shall have over it the stone of Gwynedd, a beautiful rock Jewels from the hillside, thin tiles he will give to my new house . . .*

Those 'jewels' were slates. In the 19th century, North Wales became famous for the production of high-quality roofing slates and one of the main centres grew up close to the little village of Ffestiniog. As the quarries expanded to meet demand, so the quarrying communities also grew. Blaenau Ffestiniog developed rapidly during the century – in 1801 the population was just 732 rising to over 11,000 by the early years of this century. By 1880 there were 18 places of worship in the town, with nonconformity dominating religion and liberal radicalism being the strongest political impulse.

The town was surrounded by slate quarries and mines. Only 25-30 per cent of rock removed was usable and now massive sculptural piles of waste slate dominate the landscape.

## Conwy

Conwy is one of the most impressive walled towns in Wales. Work began on the castle and town in 1283 and within four years the castle was virtually complete. This impressive achievement indicates the strategic importance of the estuary crossing, which gave access into the heartland of Welsh resistance against English encursion. The town's charter was granted in 1284 and the walls were more or less complete by 1286.

The town has been transformed by the opening of the A55 road tunnel beneath the River Conwy, which now takes heavy traffic out of the town's narrow gateways and streets.

Before 1826, travellers entered the town from the east, crossing at a point where the river swirls and speeds through a narrow gap. It was Thomas Telford who crossed this gap with his suspension bridge, which was opened on 2 July that year. It was reported that 'not the slightest accident happened with the exception of a few broken windows at the Public Houses'.

Alongside Telford's bridge is the work of the Stephensons, whose tubular-section railway bridge was opened in 1848.

## Cadair Idris

Tradition holds that the great corrie basin near the summit of Cadair Idris is the chair of a giant who lived on the mountain, and that anyone spending a night in the chair will wake the following morning either a poet or mad.

Reverend Francis Kilvert, a 19th-century diarist, climbed Cadair Idris on 13 June 1871 'The sun was shining on the hills below, but the mist crawled down and wrapped us as if in a shroud blotting out everything. The mists and clouds began to sweep by us in white thin ghostly sheets as if some great dread Presences and Powers were going past and we could only see the skirts of their white garments . . . It is an awful place in a storm. I thought of Moses on Sinai.'

Cadair Idris, at 904m (2,967ft), is one of the highest mountains in North Wales, but it appears higher still because of its precipitous sides and jagged peaks. From the top, the views can be superb, either towards Tal-y-llyn or into the Dysynni valley. The mountain may look formidable but many paths lead to its summit, and it is now a popular excursion with walkers.

## Llyn Tegid
*Bala*

The largest lake in Wales at just over 7.25km (4½ miles), Llyn Tegid forms part of the great Bala fault, a trench that runs from Towyn to Bala. The lake has an important place in the legends that are associated with water. It is said, for example, that the River Dee flows through the lake without mingling with the lake water.

The lake is reputed to have increased in size because a local well-keeper forgot to close the lid of a well. This incurred the wrath of the spirit that dwelt in the well, who caused the water to pour forth and flood the neighbouring village. At low water, the ruins of the houses are said to appear.

Richard Fenton's description in 1816 still holds true to a large extent today: '. . . a beautiful expanse of water, varies its appearance every half hour. Early it has a calm glassy surface, reflecting most distinctly the inverted Landscape . . . the horizon finely gilded. It was a School for a Painter. A small Moon appeared.'

The lake is also one of the few known habitats of the very rare small transparent fish known as gwyniad.

The earliest evidence of life in Wales has been found at Pontnewydd cave in limestone cliffs high above the Elwy valley near Denbigh. Here, archaeologists have uncovered tools made from animal bones, and traces of human bone and teeth from several individuals. They were found in the deeper recesses of the cave, having probably been carried inside by mud flows. It seems likely that the dwelling area to the front of the cave has been lost with glacial action and subsequent weathering, leaving the question of how much material and information has been lost.

The finds have been dated to 220,000 BC, making them among the oldest in Europe, and the cave may have been occupied during one of the warmer periods in the Ice Age when animals would have roamed in the valley below.

As the glaciers receded, the climate became warmer and wetter, tree cover increased and plant and animal life flourished. New technologists took advantage of rich deposits of lead and copper in the area. Halkyn mountain, south of Holywell, has been worked for minerals for more than 3,000 years and an analysis of the Acton Park hoard of Bronze Age weapons shows that lead from the mountain was introduced into the manufacturing process to improve the 'flow' of metal, setting a technological trend that was to be followed throughout Europe.

The same deposits were exploited by the Romans, who also established a tile-making works near Holt. The influence of their base at Chester was powerful and one of their many roads ran southwards to Caerleon, marking a boundary that was to be hotly contested in later centuries. Besides evidence in the landscape, the language of Wales also assimilated a number of Latin words – braich, ffenestr and eglwys (arm, window and church) are a few examples.

The border lands between Wales and England are scattered with the remains of the movement and conflict that accompanied the emergence of the two nations as separate entities. The division is clearly marked by the series of dykes built between the 7th and 9th centuries. It may be of significance that the ditches are found mainly on the western sides and, in places, the top of the bank from the bottom of the ditch is more than 2.75m (9ft) high. Offa's Dyke is now a long-distance footpath of more than 185km (177 miles). The first sections were opened in 1971 as a result of the efforts of the Offa's Dyke

Association, a group that has been responsible for encouraging a greater interest in the history and archaeological potential of the massive earthwork.

The principal town of the North East is Wrexham, now a busy commercial centre. It has grown from a market town that served the surrounding area, and the modern roads follow the early routes that radiated from the town. Its position at the edge of the agriculturally rich Cheshire plain and the uplands to the west gave the town strategic and commercial advantages.

It is thought that Wrexham has Saxon origins – Wryghtesham, the place of the smith or perhaps referring to a surname. The border area was hotly contested, with control passing backwards and forwards between the Welsh and the English. South of Wrexham is Bangor-on-Dee, the site of a once large and important monastery that housed more than 2,000 monks. The church and monastery were destroyed in 615 by Aethelfrith, King of Northumbria, who ordered the slaughter of more than a thousand monks and others who were gathered there for prayer.

The caption to Samuel and Nathaniel Buck's 1748 print of the town records that it was 'a Large well built town in the County of Denbigh, being a place of Great Resort and good Accommodation'. This was a picture that was to change as the surrounding area expanded during the 18th and 19th centuries and local coal measures and other minerals were exploited on a large scale. By the mid 19th century, inspectors of the General Board of Health saw conditions in the town that they likened to 'a camp of American Pawnee Indians'. The area around Wrexham became dominated by industry as coal and metal mining developed and iron and steel works were opened and enlarged. Ruabon and Buckley emerged as a major brick- and tile-making locality, and places such as Rhosllannerchrugog became archetypal mining communities. Although close to powerful English influence, the small town is still a concentration of Welsh language.

To the west of the Clwydian range, the fertile Vale of Clwyd marks a division. The river Clwyd rises in hills and forests above the Brenig reservoir and is fed by many tributaries as it flows below the ancient town of Denbigh and through St Asaph. The harsh treatment experienced by John Rowlands in the St Asaph workhouse was too much for him to bear, so, in 1854, aged thirteen, he ran away. He eventually found his way to New Orleans, where he was adopted by a rich cotton broker named Stanley. In gratitude, John took the surname of his benefactor and after fighting on the Confederate side in the American Civil War became a journalist. He has entered the history books as the person who uttered the words 'Dr Livingstone, I presume'. Daniel Defoe thought the Vale of Clwyd 'a most fruitful, populous, and delicious vale, full of villages and towns, the fields shining with corn, just ready for the reapers, the meadows green and flowery, and a fine river, with a mild and gentle stream running through it: nor is it a small or casual intermission, but we had the prospect of the country open before us, for above some twenty miles in length, and from 5 to 7 miles in breadth, all smiling with the same kind of complexion.'

As the railways pushed westwards along the northern coast, so a few of the small fishing villages developed into popular holiday resorts, attracting large numbers of people from the industrial Midlands and north of England. The holiday towns have a strong common identity, with their fine Victorian and Edwardian buildings and decorative ironwork. To the south, an earlier but nonetheless effective means of communication opened up the country inland as far as Newtown. The Montgomery canal system – comprising four canals – was linked to the Shropshire Union canal at Welsh Frankton. The main purpose of the canal was to provide an outlet for lime for agriculture, although it also carried general cargoes, including textiles from the manufacturing factories in Newtown and Welshpool. The fast flowing rivers were harnessed to provide power for the weaving looms and, for a period in the 19th century, the area was known as the 'Leeds of Wales' as large factories were built to accommodate the machinery. The towns that grew rapidly were indeed industrial centres even though they were small in scale. Their architecture is demonstrative of the wealth that was generated by the industry, with some very fine houses facing the main streets. Before the factories, the hand looms were usually located on the second floor of the weavers' houses. A number of these houses survive and can be easily recognised by the lines of windows on the top stories taking advantage of the natural light. Newtown, noted as the birthplace of Robert Owen the political reformer, was the main centre of manufacture and it was there in 1859 that Pryce Jones established the first mail-order business. One of its advertising leaflets of 1878 carried the verse:

*Man owes a double debt to flannel white*
*His vest by day, his blanket warm by night;*
*The prop of life in each succeeding stage,*
*The nurse of youth, and comforter of age;*
*His first best garb when hurry'd from the womb,*
*And his last robe to shroud him in the tomb.*

## Pont Fawr,
### *Llanrwst*

The River Conwy winds a leisurely route along the valley and disgorges into the estuary alongside Conwy Castle. With its large catchment area, the river is prone to flooding, so early travellers were grateful for the high, elegant stone arches that span the river at Llanrwst. Pont Fawr (big bridge) was constructed in 1636 and, at the time, was the only crossing between Llanrwst and the sea. The bridge has been attributed to Inigo Jones. Although this cannot be confirmed, the bridge is so different in design from others in the locality that such an attribution would not be surprising. Whoever was responsible for the design, the outcome is a pleasure to the eye as it sweeps over the river in three segmental arches. Its smooth, paved surface must have provided brief but pleasant relief from the appalling roads in the area. Sir Richard Wynne of Gwydir described the road from Llanrwst to Llanberis as 'the devil's bowling green'.

During the Owain Glyn Dŵr uprising, the town was so affected that the population deserted, grass grew in the streets and deer grazed freely among the houses.

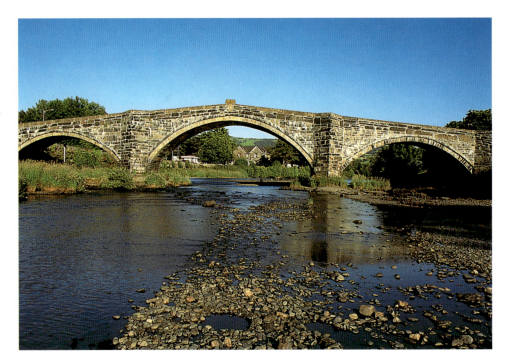

## Long Mountain
### *Nr Welshpool*

The aptly named Long Mountain runs for about 6.5km (4 miles) above the ancient town of Welshpool and looks westwards across Wales and eastwards into England. It lies at the heart of the Marches, a named derived from the old French *marche*, which means border. The Long Mountain marks the boundary between the two countries.

It was on and around the mountain that Henry Tudor met with armies from Wales who were to help him win the Battle of Bosworth Field. He landed at Milford Haven on the 3 August 1485 and marched through Wales gathering support. Near Machynlleth he approached Dafydd Llwyd, a bard, and asked for a prophesy on the likelihood of victory. Wisely, Dafydd consulted his wife who recommended that a great victory should be forecast because, she argued: 'If he wins he will not forget you. If he loses you can forget him.'

After his victory, Henry repaid the help he had received from Wales by granting titles and appointing bishoprics to a number of Welshmen. Dafydd Seisyllt became a royal bodyguard and his grandson, William Cecil, the name having been anglicized, was advisor to Queen Elizabeth I.

## Montgomery

On 30 September 1223, a day before his 16th birthday, King Henry III arrived at Montgomery and was shown 'a suitable spot for the erection of an impregnable castle'. A fortification of timber was erected in a matter of weeks, and by 1226 a stone castle was in place.

The town grew below the castle and was granted its Royal Charter in 1227 and was enclosed by a wall and ditch. Since that time, Montgomery has been essentially an 'English' town in both language and appearance.

Although Georgian architecture predominates, behind the façades and in the back gardens traces of earlier buildings are found. The town hall, built in 1748, looks down over Broad Street, which served as the main marketplace during the town's heyday in the 18th and 19th centuries.

Pevsner describes the roofs of St Nicholas Church as its 'structural glory'. The church was first mentioned in 1227 and has undergone some additions and alterations, including fine 15th-century stalls and misericords. In the churchyard is a patch of ground where grass is said never to grow. It is the burial place of John Newton Davies, wrongly convicted and hanged in 1821.

## Gregynog
*Nr Newtown*

From a distance, Gregynog looks like a classic example of a Border half-timbered house built of traditional materials. Closer inspection reveals that the black and white work is made of concrete. It hides earlier interiors, including panelling dating from 1636. Some of the estate houses and the village school are also made of concrete.

The estate was bought by Gwendoline and Margaret Davies, daughters of coal owner and railway builder David Davies of Llandinam. They created a centre for cultural activities at Gregynog and many notable musicians performed in its concert hall, including Edward Elgar. The sisters are among the most important benefactors of the National Museums & Galleries of Wales in Cardiff, having given to the museum their world-famous collection of Impressionist and Post-Impressionist paintings.

Another of their innovations was the creation of the Gregynog Press, which produced a series of limited-edition works of high quality. The press was restarted in 1975 by the University of Wales, which now runs Gregynog as an educational centre.

## Powis Castle
*Welshpool*

Powis Castle dates from the 13th century and in 1587 it became the home of Sir Edward Herbert, whose son, William, was created Baron Powis in 1629. The family remain in occupation to this day.

In the 17th century the terraces, with their balustrade and statuary, were probably created by the Dutch architect William Winde, who visited the castle in 1697 and incorporated an orangery in the terraces. In the late 18th century, William Eames's scheme to blow up the terraces and replace them with smooth, grassed slopes was rejected.

Below the terraces, the gardens sweep away into woodland and a formal water garden. Dominating the garden are the massive, clipped yews that are wall-like in their size and density. It says much for the efforts of successive generations of the family,and latterly the National Trust, that Powis is in such good condition. A visitor in 1798 said that: 'This venerable castle is going fast to decay. The buildings are in a state of dilapidation; the garden and grounds are neglected and the pride and ornament of the park is being removed for the sake of the timber.'

## Offa's Dyke

Giraldus Cambrensis in his travels through Wales in 1188 spoke of King Offa, ruler of Mercia from 757 to 796 'who by a long and extensive dyke separated the British from the English'. Perhaps he was merely repeating the words of Bishop Asser writing at the end of the 9th century about Offa 'who commanded a great bank to be built between Britain and Mercia all the way from sea to sea'. To say that the dyke is a magnificent feat of engineering is an under-statement. Running from the Severn estuary near Chepstow to the Dee estuary near Holywell, the earthwork crosses some of the loveliest scenery, through valleys, across hills, sometimes visible as a steep bank and ditch, at other places a barely discernible line.

Parts of the dyke form the boundary between Wales and England, a zone hotly contested throughout history with raiding parties and armies confronting each other across its route. Even today, people living either side often give their birthplace with precision thereby determining their nationality.

## Bodnant Garden
*Nr Conwy*

To stand on the slopes above the River Conwy and admire the view is perhaps pleasure enough in itself, but to stand and look over Bodnant Garden is to double that pleasure.

The choice of siting for the garden is inspirational, with the sloping ground carefully utilized to provide a rich variety of views. The garden has so much to offer – from close, wooded dells to Italianate terraces with a canal overlooked by a 1740 Pin Mill, which was originally built for a house in Gloucestershire but was moved to Bodnant in 1938. The garden, famous for its laburnum walk, is usually at its best from the end of May to mid June when the pergola is festooned with thousands of *Laburnum watereri* 'Vossili'.

The garden was extended about a hundred years ago by Lord and Lady Aberconway, and the family are still closely involved there. Continuity is important in dealing with gardens and Bodnant has had the benefit of more than 70 years of attention by the Puddle family of gardeners. Bodnant is owned by the National Trust.

## Pistyll Rhaeadr

At 73m (240ft) above sea level, the waterfall is the highest in Wales and has long been a place of significance for visitors. George Borrow visited in 1854 and as he approached along the narrow winding road 'saw something at a great distance, which looked like a strip of grey linen hanging over a crag . . . Closer inspection revealed water falling so gracefully, so much like thin beautiful threads.' His pleasure was marred by the natural arch, which he thought an 'unsightly object' and that it 'would be a desecration of nature to remove . . . but no one could regret if nature in one of her floods were to sweep it away'. It was listed in a poem celebrating the 'Seven Wonders of Wales':

*Pistyll Rhaeadr and Wrexham Steeple,*
*Snowdon's mountain without its people;*
*Overton yew trees, St Winifred's Wells,*
*Llangollen bridge and Gresford Bells*

The nearest village to the falls is Llanrhaeadr-ym-Mochnant (Church of the Waterfall). Bishop William Morgan, translator of the Bible into Welsh, was born here in about 1540.

## Pentrefoelas

The village of Pentrefoelas has undergone a revival in recent years, with the re-establishment of some of the crafts that were practised there in the 19th century. A poem of 1857 encapsulates the interdependency and self-sufficiency of the rural societies:

*In, 'Pentref y Foelas, in order,*
*  we see*
*Vocations, the number of forty*
*  less three;*
*They exist all together, all*
*  pleasant, serene,*
*Although of the dwellings there*
*  are but seventeen;*
*Publican, shopkeeper, for stranger*
*  and kith,*
*A draper, a farmer, a saddler*
*  and smith,*
*A labourer, gravedigger, carpenter*
*  of skill,*
*A baker, a barber and 'the man*
*  of the mill.'*

The village lies alongside the A5 road to Holyhead and was a stopping place for travellers *en route* for Ireland before the railways. It was part of the estate of C W G Wynne, who provided the finance for a schoolroom and gave allotment land to the villagers.

In 1987, a regeneration project started to improve the economy of the village by restoring the buildings, providing workshops and creating a heritage trail.

## Erddig
### *Nr Wrexham*

Erddig was one of the largest rescue operations undertaken by the National Trust at the time of its acquisition in 1973. The house had suffered from years of neglect and subsidence, and both wet and dry rot had taken their toll.

It was, however, a place worth saving because of its history, elegance and contents. The Yorke family had occupied the house for more than 250 years, and hardly anything had been thrown away. There is a rare and precious state bed of 1720, and tools and equipment used by the small army of servants. In fact, the servants had been given a very special place in the history of Erddig, the family having written about them, sometimes in verse form, and had their portraits painted. Inscribing the portrait of Edward Prince the carpenter, aged 75, in 1792 is the following:

*A Raiser this indeed of Houses*
*That has already had four*
*  Spouses,*
*And if the Present, don't survive*
*Hopes to rebuild them up to five*
*From these bold strokes*
*Of Princes, to adorn the place*
*Who thrive beneath their parent*
*  stock, and make good chips from*
*  that old block.*

## Rhug Chapel
### Nr Corwen

The chapel, recently repaired and conserved by Cadw, is exquisite. The interior is a rare example of a 16th-century chapel that has largely survived the alterations and improvements much loved by the Victorians.

A private chapel, Rhug was built by Colonel William Salisbury, Governor of Denbigh Castle. The Cadw guidebook refers to the deed of endowment in which Colonel Salisbury would appoint 'a discreet and competently learned scholar of good carriage and behaviour, being a distinct and sensible reader, and being a minister and within Holy Orders . . . to officiate therein, and to read and celebrate Divine Service and other Holy exercises therein in both the native and vulgarly known tongue there.'

The roof is richly carved and decorated with angels positioned at the bases of two of the roof trusses, which are carved with a flowing floral design. A 17th-century wall painting depicts the transience of life and the permanence of death in a series of inscriptions. One reads 'pob cadarn: gwan i ddiwedd' (every strong one is weak in the end). The benches are carved with creatures, both real and fanciful, including dragons and a wyvern.

## Llyn Fyrnwy

Llyn Fyrnwy is not technically a lake but a reservoir, having been constructed by the Liverpool Corporation in the 1880s to supply water to the conurbation. Its completion transformed a remote, upland valley with its scattered covering of trees, into a scene more reminiscent of the Rhineland. The water's surface stretches for more than 8km (5 miles) and is lined by thickly planted conifers. Beyond the trees, the open, rolling hills of the Berwyn Mountains reach far into the distance.

The dam is one of the earliest large masonry structures to be built in Britain. It is 358m (1,175ft) long and 44m (145ft) high, and is constructed of blocks weighing as much as ten tons set in hard mortar. It is a gravity dam that relies on its sheer mass and weight to hold it in position. Drainage systems in the foundations can be opened to release pressure. Water tapped from the reservoir takes 48 hours to travel the 113-km (70-mile) conduit to Liverpool. The fairy-tale landscape is enhanced by the water-straining tower with its soaring roof. The estate includes a reserve for the Royal Society for the Protection of Birds.

## Castell Dinas Brân
### Nr Llangollen

*When rising slow from Deva's
    wizard streams the blue mists,
    borne on the autumnal gale,
Cloud the deep windings of
    Llangollen vale,
And the high cliff glows with the
    day's latest gleam;
Dinas, while on thy brow in
    pensive dream
Reclined, no sounds of earth my
    ear assail,
I bid the ancient chiefs of Britain
    hail*

(Sonnet XI, *On Castle Dinas
Brân*, W Sotheby, 1794)

The Iron Age hill fort of Dinas
Brân overlooks the Vale of
Llangollen and is a familiar
silhouette above the town. The
bank and ditch of the early fortification are clearly visible even
though part of the fort is covered
by the remains of a medieval
castle. The medieval fortifications
date from about 1270 and were
built by Madog, a local prince.
Its defensive strength was never
tested in direct attack, but the
garrison deserted and burned it in
1277 when faced by the powerful
armies of Edward I.

   The backdrop to Dinas Brân is
equally spectacular, where the
steep cliffs of Creigiau Eglwyseg
are formed of bands of limestone.

## Denbigh

The town lies at the heart of the
Vale of Clwyd. The fertile valley,
with its easy access from the
coast, made it a prime target for
the English advance into Wales
during the Middle Ages. Denbigh
sat at the centre of one of the
hotly contested areas.

   Edward I took the town and
castle from Dafydd ap Gruffudd
on 16 October 1280. The
development of the town from
that point onwards exemplified
the normal practice of creating a
'plantation' where, behind the
town wall and under the protection of the castle, an 'English'
town developed with its markets
and charters.

   During the Civil War, Charles I
stayed three days at the castle in
late September 1645. The following year, the castle withstood a
three-month siege, which ended
after the garrison realized how
isolated they were with little
hope of relief. An entry in the
Articles of Surrender stated that:
'. . . if an officer, soldier, or p'sons
w'soever, be sicke or wounded
soe they cannot at p'sent enjoy
the benefitt of these articles, y't
shall have libertie to stay at
Denbigh untill they be recover'd.'

## Great Orme Copper Mines
*Llandudno*

Wales has a long history of metal mining and one of the earliest sites is located on the Great Orme, above Llandudno. It is a massive outcrop of carboniferous limestone with a series of copper-bearing lodes. The area was worked intensively during the 18th and 19th centuries, but archaeological investigation over the past 20 years has revealed evidence of large-scale activity since the Bronze Age.

Such has been the extent of the discoveries that the Great Orme Mine Company has opened the workings to visitors. During excavations, more than 26,000 bone tools have been found, made mostly from cattle, pigs and sheep. They were used to work the softer rocks and deposits while a large number of hammer stones used for the harder places have also been discovered.

The geological conditions enabled early miners to work in comparative safety, since the ore veins lay against the hard limestone, making tunnel supports unnecessary. The site is proving to be of a scale previously unknown in the Bronze Age in Britain, and it must have been one of the principal copper-producing areas.

## St Dyfiog's Church,
*Llanrhaeadr-yng-Nghinmeirch*

St Dyfiog's Church has a rare example of a complete Jesse window dating from 1553. It survived the depredations of the Civil War by being dismantled, placed in the parish chest and buried for safekeeping until it was re-erected in 1661. Richard Fenton, the antiquary, visited the church on Saturday, 17 September 1808 and was told of the vault where 'a box lined with flannel, containing only the head of a Man, supposed to be that of Captain Wynne in the time of the Civil War', had been discovered.

There is a flamboyant baroque memorial of 1702 to Maurice Jones of Llanrhaeadr Hall, who, according to the inscription: '. . . was a Gentleman of a most respectable family, the existent heir male of the ancient house of Gwydir, of amiable manners and a benevolent disposition, qualities which endeared him to his Friends, and made the loss the deepest affliction to his widow.' *Archaeologia Cambrensis*, the Journal of the Cambrian Archaeological Association, in 1884, refers to the church having undergone a thorough restoration, which was completed on 20 April 1880.

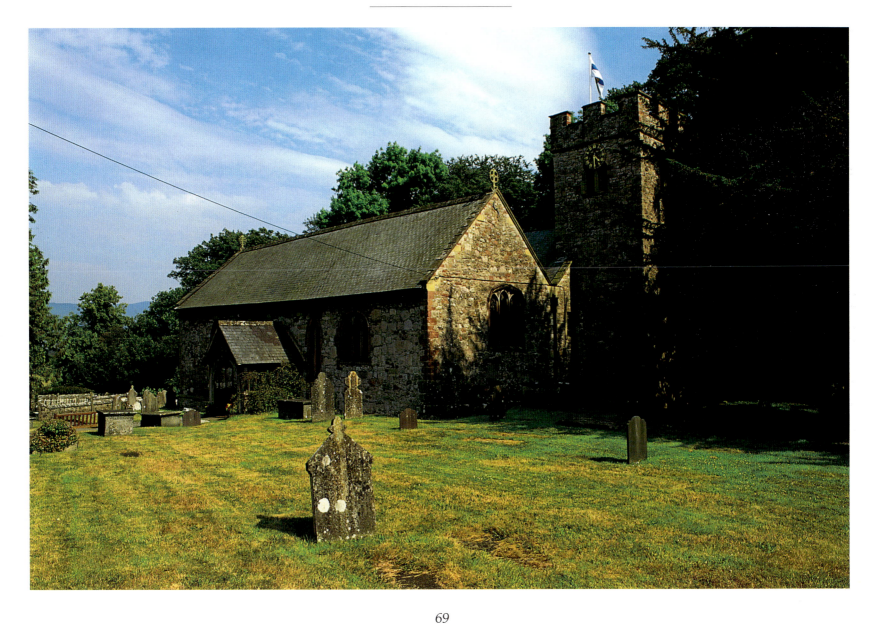

## Capel Garmon
*Nr Betws-y-coed*

The neolithic chambered tomb was built about 5,500 years ago and is similar in design and construction to a series of structures in the Cotswold and River Severn regions. Recent research, aided by carbon dating, indicates that burials may have taken place there over a 500-year period. It was thought that such tombs were reserved for privileged members of society, but it now seems likely that they were communal burial chambers.

There is little doubt that the tomb was disturbed before the first of the modern-day excavations in 1924 produced a fragment of neolithic pot as well as pieces of 'Beaker' pottery from the early Bronze Age (about 2400-1400 BC). The Cadw guide to the site refers to a description by Edward Lhuyd in 1699, *Karnedd vawr hir o Gerrig ond bod daiar gewdi tyvy drosty* (a great and long cairn made of stones, but covered with earth). The earth covering has long since disappeared but the work of the neolithic builders is still visible. Not far from Capel Garmon an ornate iron fire-dog (c. 1-50 AD) was discovered in a bog in 1852. It is now in the National Museums & Galleries of Wales in Cardiff.

## Llandudno

A guidebook to North Wales published in 1895 complained 'the great drawback of Llandudno, we have said, is the want of protection from the rays of the summer sun'. The land on which the town developed, from the mid 19th century, was owned by the Mostyn family, who took great care to ensure that developers were subject to restrictions dictating the type of house to be built in different parts of the town. Large buildings with gardens were built close to the sea, and smaller houses were built inland. As the century progressed, so the town developed as a seaside resort.

'Modest lodgings, consisting of a sitting room and bedroom, can be found a little way from the shore, for thirty shillings to two pounds a week; and the terms go up to eight or ten guineas for a suite of three or four rooms on the Parade.'

Llandudno is one of the best examples of a Victorian town in Wales. The pier was opened in 1876 and the funicular railway to the top of the Great Orme was opened in 1906. It was in the town that Charles Dodgson, under his pen-name of Lewis Carroll, began work on *Alice in Wonderland*.

## St Winifred's Well
*Holywell*

The well is dedicated to Winifred, daughter of a 7th-century prince. Being very beautiful, she attracted the attention of Cracdocus, a prince, who tried to seduce her. Furious at being rejected, he beheaded Winifred and, according to Thomas Pennant, writing in 1778, 'a spring of uncommon size burst forth from the place where the head had rested'.

Winifred's uncle, St Beuno, retrieved her head and 'joined it nicely to the body, which instantly reunited. The place was only visible by a slender white line encircling her neck.'

The first pilgrimage was recorded in 1115 and the well has drawn visitors ever since. The walls of the chapel are covered with names, initials and dates.

Until mining close to the source diminished the flow in 1917, it was estimated that six million gallons of water flowed from the well every minute. In 1240, the church and well were granted to the 12th-century Basingwerk Abbey. St Winifred's Chapel dates from the 15th century but has been much altered. St James's Church alongside was rebuilt in 1769-70. A visitor in 1720 noted that by 'the side of the well there grows a sweet scented moss, much esteemed by Pilgrims'.

## Froncysyllte Aqueduct
*Nr Llangollen*

Work on the Shropshire Union canal towards Llangollen was started in 1793 to give access into the industrial areas around Ruabon and Wrexham. To get there involved crossing the deep and wide valley of the River Dee at Froncysyllte.

The engineer engaged for the task was Thomas Telford. To avoid the construction of an expensive and complex system of locks he decided to cross the valley on a slender aqueduct made of cast-iron sections mounted on stone pillars. His work is still a most remarkable feat of engineering and narrow boats are carried 38.5m (127ft) above the river in a trough more than 304m (1,000ft) long.

Sir Walter Scott described it as the 'most impressive work of art I have ever seen'. The opening of the aqueduct was a great occasion with more than 8,000 people '. . . stationed all around us, from the tops of the mountain to the banks of the Dee, and were cheering and exulting, with intervals of silent astonishment'.

The Horseshoe Falls on the River Dee at Llangollen are actually a massive weir built to provide water for the canal.

## Halkyn
*Nr Holywell*

Lead has been mined in Wales since prehistoric times, and the Romans operated smelting works in Flintshire. One of the most productive areas were the deposits at Halkyn Mountain above Holywell. In 1818 the Grosvenor family of Eaton Hall in Cheshire began work on the great level, which was still being lengthened in 1901 when it had reached a distance of 8km (5 miles).

Their objective was to drain the extensive workings and ore deposits in Halkyn Mountain and it was well worth the investment. In the first half of the 18th century mines in the area produced a profit of £360,000 over a period of 20 years.

The surface of the hills above Rhes-y-cae are pockmarked with the pits and depressions of centuries of mining. There were hundreds of shafts sunk. Many have collapsed but others have been capped by a 'beehive' of stones – a technique that was introduced from Derbyshire.

This is a landscape of small, scattered communities with groups of houses clustered around a pub and sometimes a tiny school. Lead mining in the area declined in the 19th century as cheaper imports proved to be too competitive.

## Valle Crucis
*Nr Llangollen*

The 'Valley of the Cross' is a direct reference to the Pillar of Eliseg, a 9th-century cross that stands a short distance from the Cistercian Abbey of Valle Crucis.

The abbey was founded on 28 January 1201 by Madog ap Gruffudd Maelor, and its siting exemplifies so much that the Cistercian order considered important. Their abbeys were invariably placed in remote areas and were usually austere places. They were the centres of local economies and the monks of Valle Crucis cared for extensive areas of arable and grazing land. Their churches were built to standard plans, with the layouts dominated by long naves. Decorative features are few at Valle Crucis, those that exist are of good quality, including some carved corbels and the delightful tracery of a rose window.

After the Dissolution, parts of the abbey were converted into a dwelling and, in the course of repairing or enlarging one of the fireplaces, an exquisitely decorated grave slab has been used to support the chimney breast.

Richard Fenton thought the Abbey 'undoubtedly as fine a specimen of Masonry as any Monastick building Wales can produce'.

## Chirk Castle Gates

The gates at Chirk Castle are one of the best examples of ornamental ironwork in Europe. They were commissioned by Sir Richard Myddelton, owner of the castle, in 1711 from the Davies family of the Croes Foel foundry, a short distance from the iron-making centre of Bersham. Two members of the family stand out as consummate craftsmen – Robert born in 1675 and John who was baptized in 1683.

The brothers produced a number of gates for the locality, and these have been described in Ifor Edwards's book on the Davies brothers.

The commission was completed before Sir Richard died in 1716 but the brothers continued to work for the estate, producing further gates and railings. They were paid at the rate of 2 shillings per day and an account dated 10 January 1711 records: 'Expenses for Drinks to the Forge-men by giving them orders to draw the iron for the new gates.'

The castle is one of Edward 1's chain of fortifications, completed in 1310. Until the 16th century, it was occupied by a succession of owners. It came to Sir Thomas Myddelton in 1589, and the family has lived there ever since.

## Wrexham Church

The graveyard of St Giles Church in Wrexham has a memorial to Elihu Yale, the benefactor of Yale University where, as a tribute to him, a replica of the church tower stands. Elihu Yale was born in Boston in 1648 but his family came from the Wrexham area. One of their houses was Plas yn Iâl, from which the name Yale is derived. He was governor of the East India Company and in 1718 he was asked to help the then struggling college. He did so by sending them a portrait of George I, which now hangs in the university art gallery, and £200 in sterling. In 1721 he sent a cargo of textiles and books, which were sold and raised £562/12 shillings.

In further recognition, Yale paid for the refurbishment of his tomb in 1871 on which is inscribed the following: *Born in America, in Europe bred, In Africa travelled and in Asia wed.*

The church was virtually rebuilt after a fire in 1463. The tower, for which Pevsner considers the church 'justly famous', is inscribed 1506, but wills of 1518 and 1520 indicate that work was still in progress. It is one of the best examples of Perpendicular architecture in Wales, richly decorated and rising in five stages to 41.5m (136ft).

## Rhuddlan Castle

In March 1284 Edward I proclaimed the Statute of Rhuddlan, which set in place administrative boundaries that remained until 1974. The castle is located at an important strategic point a few miles inland from the North Wales coast, at the entrance to the fertile Vale of Clwyd.

Edward's incursions into North Wales depended on a constant supply of goods by sea. Rhuddlan was the headquarters for his campaign against Llywelyn ap Gruffudd, and to ensure good access from the sea the meandering River Clwyd was canalized over some 4.8km (3 miles). It was an outstanding example of civil engineering for the time and took more than three years to finish. Today, 700 years on, the river still follows the same course.

It was at Rhuddlan that Edward I announced the birth of his son as a prince 'born in Wales and could speak never a word of English, whose life and conversation no man was able to staine'.

Rhuddlan was originally a Saxon foundation that was occupied by Gruffudd ap Llywelyn in 1063. Edward began building his castle on the site ten years later.

## Berwyn Mountains

Henry II mounted a full-scale invasion against Owain Gwynedd and Rhys ap Gruffudd in 1165. He gathered his army at Oswestry and entered Wales, camping at Corwen. Brut y Tywysogyon (the Chronicle of the Princes) details the encounter: 'And after staying long in their tents there and one dared not attack the other in battle, the king was greatly angered; and he moved his host into the wood of Dyffryn Ceiriog, and had the wood cut down and felled to the ground.'

Despite fierce resistance, he advanced into the Berwyn mountains where he 'was oppressed by a mighty tempest of wind and exceeding great torrents of rain'. His advance foundered and he had to return to England, his policy for controlling Wales in tatters. The route he took is still known as Heol y Saeson (Englishmen's Road).

John Ceiriog Hughes, described as 'the greatest of Welsh lyric poets' was born in 1832 at Llanarmon in the Berwyn mountains. He spent a large part of his working life as a station master and the Institute at Llansanffraid Glynceiriog commemorates him and another local poet, Huw Morris, who was born in 1622 and was known as 'Eos Ceiriog', (the nightingale of Ceiriog).

## Llangollen

Dylan Thomas turned a corner in Llangollen and saw '. . . over the bridge, come three Javanese, winged, breastplated, helmeted, carrying gongs and steel bubbles . . . Burgundian girls, wearing, on their heads, bird cages made of velvet, suddenly whisk on the pavement into a coloured dance. A Viking goes into a pub.' Every summer this delightful town plays host to the International Eisteddfod when singers, dancers and musicians from all over the world come together to compete.

The town is perfectly suited for the event. When Thomas Telford was designing the A5 road he arranged that it should bypass the town, thus preserving Llangollen from the development that probably would have followed.

Notable travellers had been entertained by the 'Ladies of Llangollen' – Lady Eleanor Butler and Miss Sarah Ponsonby – who lived at Plas Newydd on the outskirts of the town. They arrived in 1780 and, for more than 50 years, entertained a host of visitors. The Duke of Somerset toured North Wales in 1795 and thought their way of life 'preferable to all the boasted pleasures of fashionable dissipation'.

## Gwrych Castle

Gwrych Castle is a marvellous example of a 19th-century architectural and landscape folly. It is the fanciful creation of Lloyd Bamford Hesketh, who succeeded to the estate in 1816. He drew up the plans in consultation with Thomas Rickman, architect and historian, and the foundation stone was laid in 1819. Work continued at various levels of intensity until the early years of the present century. Inscriptions above the entrance gates listed historic events that took place in the vicinity.

The mansion itself is resplendent in castellations and turrets, as are the extensive walls and towers that stretch across the hillside. A late 19th-century guidebook gave details of the castle: 'The frontage of Gwrych Castle measures 480 yards, its tower is 93 feet high, and there are 17 turrets besides, which altogether make it one of the grandest and most picturesque places in North Wales.'

## Llanidloes

In the centre of Llanidloes is, according to the architectural historian Sir Nikolaus Pevsner, the only timber-framed market hall surviving in Wales. The ground floor is cobbled and open-sided. John Wesley is reputed to have preached standing on the block of stone in one corner.

Llanidloes was a textile manu-facturing town and many of the houses have well-illuminated top stories where the home workers had their looms. It was the transfer of manufacturing into large factories, combined with the rise of Chartism and the poverty experienced by many in the town, that led to the so-called riot in 1839. Police and troops were sent in by the Home Secretary and the local memory is that the mayor took refuge by hiding under his bed.

The land rises rapidly to the west of the town and the richness of the Severn river valley gives way to open upland, with its reser-voirs and remains of lead mines. A French agriculturalist visited the region in 1855 and thought that the upland areas should have been 'almost deserted by man' had it not been for the mines and quarries that resulted in 'a disproportionate agricultural development'.

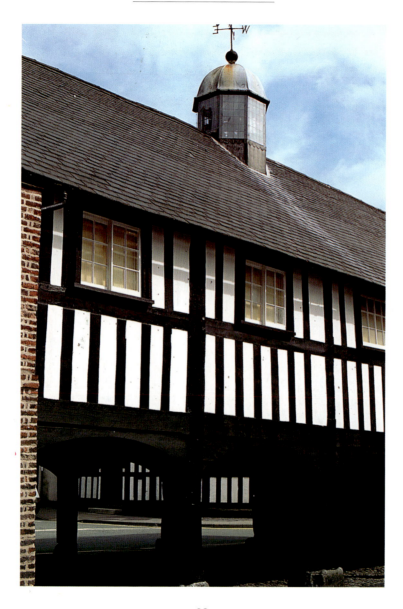

## Talerddig Cutting

One of the deepest railway cuttings in the world can be seen on one of the few remaining rural lines left in Wales. The Newtown to Machynlleth line was part of the Cambrian Railways Company system, and the first train arrived at Machynlleth on May Day of 1862. The Talerddig cutting is 35.5m (120ft) deep and when it was completed it was considered to be one of the great feats of railway engineering.

A driving force behind the rail-way was David Davies, who was born of humble origins in the small village of Llandinam. He began his working life as a sawyer and rose to become one of the most important industrialists in Wales, owning coal mines, docks and railways. He and his family were well known for their philan-thropy. David Davies was one of the main contractors building the line, working with another railway speculator, Thomas Savin.

The construction was not with-out its problems, especially at Talerddig. Here, a deep cutting was needed to take the line through a series of hard grits at the watershed between the Severn and Dyfi basins. The discovery of a new bed in the Silurian rocks was given the name Talerddig Grits.

# SOUTH WEST

**Garn Goch**

The hillforts of Wales are quite remarkable for both their number – nearly six hundred have been identified – and in some instances for their size. Their builders often utilised the natural contours of the chosen site to enhance the defensive features and constructed complex fortifications and entrances. There has been much debate as to why they should have taken so much trouble but recent research indicates that climate change limited the availability of good arable land therefore the need for clearly defined territories was vital. The hillforts became part of a system of defence against unwelcome intrusion.

To build the hillforts required a society that was cohesive and organised, probably based on a strict hierarchical tribal structure. At the time of the Roman invasion of Wales in AD 48 there were five main tribes across the country. The main period of hillfort building began about seven to eight hundred years BC and a number continued in use during the Roman period.

South West Wales is predominantly dependent on agriculture. Farming has changed in so many ways. Today the farm is more often than not an independent economic unit that can operate without too much reliance on neighbours. This was not the case in the past, when topography and society gave life a close, local focus. There was little need to travel far beyond the confines of the neighbourhood other than to fairs or markets. Mutual co-operation was vital and the farming communities were close-bonded and inter-reliant. At harvest or sheep-shearing time, people would gather from miles around to help, working from early morning until late in the evening. There was always time for relaxation, for singing and storytelling, when new tales could be added to the stock of folk lore that had been passed down through generations. In such stable communities folk traditions were maintained until well into this century.

North Pembrokeshire was famous for the game of cnapan, a ball game played by hundreds of players who would range between goals perhaps 13km (8 miles) apart. Rules were virtually non-existent and broken bones and fractured skulls were commonplace. A Pembrokeshire historian, George Owen, who lived between 1552 and 1613, was a spectator: 'It is strange to behold with what eagerness the play is followed, for in the fury of the chase they respect neither hedge, ditch, pale or wall, dale, bushes, river or rock or any other passable impediment.'

An invisible line, called the landsker, runs diagonally across Pembrokeshire from Amroth in the south to Newgale on the north-west coast. To the south is 'Little England', secured and settled by the Normans, and to the north the 'Welshry', the division marked in places by castles and by language and accents. George Owen noted in 1600 that the divide was so marked that the difference between Welsh and English speakers was not more than a pathway wide. Although not so clearly marked today, the divide between north and south in the county is still evident. The same applies to Gower, whose inhabitants can trace their ancestors to Flemings brought into the area during the medieval period as part of the process of anglicization.

In the uplands of Cardiganshire and Carmarthenshire, sheep farming is vital to the economy. The sheep in these hills have to be tough to survive and among the toughest are the Welsh mountain sheep. Their ancestry can be traced to animals brought in by the

Romans and crossbred with native species. Upland farms were small, seldom larger than 50 acres, supporting a few cattle and enough arable land to feed the family and stock. Beyond the fenced and walled boundaries were sheep runs, sometimes stretching over enormous tracts of open hillside.

During harsh winters, the flocks were taken down to lowland areas, to the hendre (the winter dwelling and main residence). The summers were spent at the hafod (the summer dwelling house), often a temporary structure that, as demand for land increased, was occupied on a full-time basis.

Although coarse, the wool was sent to the hand and machine looms in Newtown, Llanidloes and the Teifi valley. Sheep-shearing time was an opportunity for festivities as well as hard work. Farmers and farmhands from miles around would gather at a particular farm and from first light until well into the evening the shearing sheds were full of noise and activity. After work, it was a time for food, drink and relaxation, often a concert or storytelling.

Before the introduction of the railways, the drover was a link with the wider world, bringing news and hard currency in exchange for the cattle that had been sent to markets in England. Their old routes are still traceable across the open hills. The drover was an important person, since he was effectively trusted with the wealth of the farmer. The herds were walked at about 3km (2 miles) an hour to the markets. To ensure against loss of cattle and the hard cash they carried, drovers' banks were established, the first in Llandovery in 1799. Rees Prichard, who lived between 1579 and 1644, was Vicar of Llandovery. He offered poetic advice to the drover:

> If thou'rt a Dealer, honest be each act,
> And fairly pay for what to thee is sold:
> Be to thy promise and thy word exact:

The railways had a profound effect. They saw the demise of the drover and the decline of many of the small but once vitally important markets. But they also provided the means to export foodstuffs to new and larger markets. Before the railways, the sea was the main means of communication, and many farmers along the coast bought shares in ships or cargoes and younger sons signed up as sailors. In the port of New Quay, more than 200 craft were built in the 19th century to serve the coastal trade and much further afield.

The Irish Sea has long been a vital line of communication, with constant movement between Wales and Ireland since the earliest times. Evidence of these close links survives. In South West Wales and the south of Ireland are concentrations of inscribed stones dating from the 5th to 7th centuries. A number of them carry inscriptions in the Ogham alphabet, which contained 20 letters comprised of notches and strokes arranged on either side of a line. Vertical edges of the stones were used as the guidelines. At Nevern Church in North Pembrokeshire, an Ogham stone has been used as a window sill and is dedicated to the memory of 'Maglocunnus son of Clutoris'. On a remote headland beyond Cardigan is the Church of the Holy Cross at Mwnt. Simple and serene, with an air of tranquillity and peace, this is a place of great significance, a place where prayers could be offered before or after sea crossings.

The most renowned of the holy men in Wales was Dewi Sant, who established his strict ascetic order at St. David's. Many miracles were attributed to him and St David's became an important place for pilgrims. He is thought to have died on 1 March 589. Holy men moved freely between the countries, as did sometimes less welcome visitors. From the west, according to Gildas's *De Excidio Britanniae* (*The Ruin and Conquest of Britain*, c. 540) came invaders in boats made of skin 'whose hulls might be seen creeping across the glassy surface of the main like so many insects awakened from torpor by the heat of the noonday sun'. Coracles are the descendants of those ancient craft, and a few owners are still licensed to fish from them. The design of the coracle varied with the different rivers depending on the water conditions and the speed of flow. The beauty of the coracle was that it was very light and easily repaired, an important attribute in some of the rocky rivers of South west Wales. Some fishermen carried a tub of lard with them as a temporary repair kit for tears in the fabric covering.

In the museum at Carmarthen there is a verse referring to the coracles used on the River Tywi:

> *Upon the glittering stream below,*
> *Those fishermen of courage bold*
> *In numerous pairs, pursue their trade*
> *In coracles themselves have made;*
> *Form'd of slight twigs with flannel cas'd*
> *O'er which three coats of tar are plac'd*
> *And (as each porter bears his pack)*
> *Each mounts his vessel on his back.*

Coracles are still used and powered by a single paddle, they sweep seemingly effortlessly over the water – a living link with a distant past.

## St David's Cathedral

St David, the patron saint of Wales, established a monastic settlement at a site near the present cathedral in the 6th century. It was a strict order, which considered work to be fundamental to religious life, according to Rhigyfarch's *Vita Davidis*, written more than 500 years after David's death. The monks were known as the Aquati, the Watermen, because they drank only water in preference to wine. They lived on a diet of bread and vegetables and everything was held in common. Great emphasis was placed on caring for the poor.

The location of the settlement was important, lying close to the sea for good communication yet in a sheltered hollow where crops could be grown and animals reared away from the westerly winds. St David was canonized in 1120 and St David's became an important place of pilgrimage. Two pilgrimages to St David's were considered to be equal to one to Rome. The cathedral was dedicated in 1131 and later rebuilt and enlarged. Restoration and alterations continued until this century.

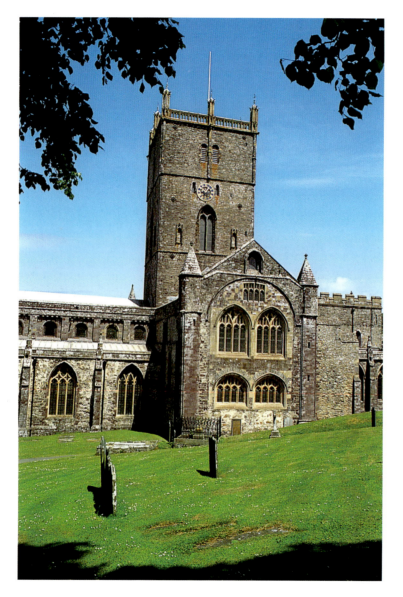

## Hafod
### Nr Aberystwyth

Hafod was the creation of the visionary Thomas Johnes, who began to build his paradise in 1783. He spent a fortune on hundreds of thousands of trees, building roads and bridges and literally blasting away parts of the hills to create vistas and gardens.

The result was a landscape that became famous and attracted many visitors, including Samuel Coleridge and J M W Turner. Some of the lines from *Kubla Khan* are thought to refer to Hafod:

> *And here were gardens bright*
> *with sinuous rills,*
> *Where blossomed many an*
> *incense-bearing tree;*
> *And here were forests ancient as*
> *the hills,*
> *Enfolding sunny spots of greenery*

Thomas Johnes and his wife, Jane, doted on their daughter Mariamne, who they described as being 'dearer than the light'. She was a delightful, talented girl who grew to be an intelligent, capable woman with a wide range of interests, especially her personal garden. She died tragically early, a few days after her 27th birthday.

The house, part of which was designed by John Nash, was demolished in 1955 but the landscape remains.

**Abergwesyn**

The wild, sparsely populated
country north of Llanwrtyd Wells
has been described as the last
wilderness in Wales. It is the land
of the red kite, spiralling skylarks
and the occasional glimpse of a
peregrine falcon. It was once
home to wolves, and Camddwr
Bleiddiad (the Wolf's Leap) is
one of the loneliest places. The
open, rolling hills punctuated by
isolated, wind-stunted trees
generate an overwhelming feeling
of solitude.

Such places are now prized as
an alternative to the pressures of
modern urban life. In 1599 this
area was described as being 'harsh
unforgiving land'. Life was hard
for those trying to eke out a living
from thin, upland soils: '. . . the
air there is sharp and cold . . . the
soil is hungry, rough and churlish
and hardly bettered for painful
labour.' Perhaps it is not too
surprising that, when alternative
lifestyles became available, the
people left this land.

This is a walker's paradise, with
roads few and far between and
the deep valleys giving way to
rocky hill tops where, on clear
days, a large part of Wales can
be viewed.

**View from the top of
Black Mountain**
*Nr Llangadog*

Northwards from the Black
Mountain stretch the rolling hills
and gentle valleys of
Carmarthenshire. This is a land
where farming is important
although there have been many
changes from the time when
farming was the keystone of the
economy. A local historian gave
a succinct context to the role of
the farmer: 'If the farmer was
poor then all the people who
depended upon him were impov-
erished as well, because in a local
rural community everything
works round the farmer; all the
craftsmen and the traders, they
were interdependent on the
farmer and if he flourished, they
flourished. The other village
down the road at one time boasted a blacksmith's shop, a village
inn, a carpenter and wheelwright,
a weaver, a thatcher and sundry
skilled labourers.'

The road that links with rural
Carmarthenshire was opened in
1833 to connect with limestone
quarries and kilns along the top
of the Black Mountain. Great
reliance was placed on lime as a
fertilizer, which was mixed with
farmyard manure.

## Nr Cwrtycadno
*Carmarthenshire*

It is possible to walk for a day in some of the Carmarthenshire valleys without seeing another person. The hillsides are often covered with hanging sessile oak woods contrasting with the open uplands. The Welsh Robin Hood, Twm Siôn Catti, who lived between 1530 and 1620, is reputed to have taken refuge in a cave in the area, and his exploits have become part of local folk legend. The writer and traveller George Borrow met a farmer during his travels in 1854 who knew the cave: 'Very queer cave it is, in strange situation: steep rock just above it, Towey river roaring below.'

The upper reaches of the River Tywi have recently become known as 'Red Kite country'. The recovery of the red kite from near extinction has been remarkable. By the early years of this century, egg collecting, indiscriminate use of poisons and hunting had taken their toll, and just one female bird produced sufficient offspring to keep the species going.

There are now around 107 nesting pairs in Wales. Their range is ever increasing, and the thinly populated lands of upland Carmarthenshire provide a perfect habitat.

## Elan Valley

The Birmingham Corporation Water Act 1892 authorized the building of a series of reservoirs along the Elan Valley to the north of Rhaeadr. Their construction changed the once-remote landscape that had so impressed Shelley when he visited the area after his expulsion from Oxford in 1811. However, there were parts he found 'gloomy and desolate'. He returned in 1812 and lived for about a year in the area with his wife, Harriet Westwood, and wrote of the 'mountains and rocks seeming to form a barrier round this great valley which the tumult of the world may never overleap'. He had not reckoned with the Victorian and Edwardian engineers.

Between 1892 and 1904 an intense period of construction resulted in the massive Elan reservoirs. These are magnificent feats of engineering in their own right, but the scale of the project is enhanced by the pipeline, 118km (73 miles) in length, which conveys the water to Birmingham.

Inevitably, the coming of the reservoirs caused displacement of the small community and the destruction of their houses, including Nant Gwyllt, once occupied by the Shelleys.

## Tregaron Bog

Tregaron Bog was formed on the site of a lake whose waters were impounded behind glacial moraine. As the flow of water cut through the moraine, so the lake gradually drained, reeds began to colonize the lake bed and, eventually, trees grew. As rainfall increased, the water level rose sufficiently to kill off the trees, thus providing the perfect habitat for sphagnum moss. This in turn provided the material from which the peat formed in the dome-shaped, raised bog. The water table is just below the surface in places, making walking a little like treading on a sponge.

The bog is maintained and managed by the Countryside Council for Wales, and it is an important habitat for plants and bird life. Some 40 species of breeding bird have been recorded, including the skylark, sedge warbler and reed bunting.

Before the bog was protected, its peat deposits formed an important source of fuel for the surrounding area. During the summer months the top soil would be removed with breast ploughs and the peat cut into strips using special, long-bladed spades and stacked in piles to await transportation.

## Constitution Hill,
*Aberystwyth*

Aberystwyth is both a resort and a university town. Thomas Savin, railway engineer and entrepreneur, began building a lavish hotel in 1864, the year the railway reached the town. Although unfinished, the hotel was opened in 1865 but the following year Savin went bankrupt and the building remained incomplete until acquired by the University of Wales, Aberystwyth in 1872. The money for the university was raised from all sectors of society. Most donations were less than 2*s* 6*d* and came from the miners and quarrymen of Wales.

The opening of the railway was a great boost to the tourist trade and the town expanded as a main destination, attracting visitors from the Midlands, the North of England and South Wales. One of Aberystwyth's attractions remains the funicular railway that climbs 122m (400ft) to the top of Constitution Hill. Opened in 1896, the railway operated on the water balance system until 1926, when it was electrified.

On another hill overlooking the town stands the National Library of Wales, which is one of the most important libraries in Britain. It contains the most complete and definitive collection of printed and written material about Wales.

## Dolaucothi
### Nr Pumsaint

The ore-bearing rocks at Dolaucothi are 438 million years old. They were subjected to massive upheavals and shearing and in areas of weakness and fractures super-heated liquids percolated upwards. The hot solutions were rich in minerals that cooled, solidified and formed the valuable deposits.

There has been much debate as to whether the deposits were worked during the Roman times, but there is no denying the archaeological evidence of a Roman fortlet under the present village of Pumsaint.

The very name of Pumsaint (five saints) has associations with mining. A large stone near the main workings is known as the saints' stone because legend refers to the concavities on its long side as being the place where pilgrims laid their heads. The stone is, in fact, an anvil on which gold-bearing rock was placed and hammered to separate the ore from the worthless rock.

The deposits were also worked from the 1870s up to the out-break of the World War II, and a large area shows evidence of mining over a long period. The site is owned by the National Trust and the underground workings are open to visitors.

## Alltcafan Textile Mill
### Pentre-cwrt

Woollen manufacturing is one of the oldest and once most important industries in Wales. Spinning and weaving took place on a part-time basis in many homes to provide cloth for the family. From the mid 18th century, the industry began to be mechanized and water power became essential to drive the wheels and machinery. This led to a concentration of activity around fast-flowing rivers and streams.

In the second half of the 19th century, a number of villages along or near the River Teifi and its tributaries became the focus of an intensive and, for a time, prosperous textile-manufacturing industry. This involved the growth of a factory system more familiar to the great manufacturing towns of northern England, but here seen on a much smaller scale. More than 50 mills operated in the area by the end of the century, supplying the rapidly growing industrial districts. Flannel shirts were worn by South Wales miners because the fabric was hard wearing and absorbed sweat. The number of mills declined after World War I as cheaper imports provided fierce competition.

## Dinefwr Park
### *Llandeilo*

A visitor to South Wales in 1794, Clutterbuck, visited Dinefwr and wrote: 'Art and nature have contributed numberless beauties to the scenery of the place, where the former has not introduced any of its formalities or the latter suffered to run luxuriantly wild.'

For years, Dinefwr was one of the great landscape secrets of Wales. Paintings on display in Newton House in the park, thought to date from 1660 and 1670, show gardens, parterres and topiary laid out around the house and depict one point in a long history of landscaping and occupation. Dinefwr is one of the ancient kingdoms of Wales, from here the rulers of Deheubarth held sway over the greater part of South Wales.

The park has a herd of deer that have been in residence since the 17th century. The White Park cattle are thought to be descendants of an ancient tribute herd referred to in the laws of Hywel Dda (Hywel the Good).

'Capability' Brown wrote to the owner after a visit in 1775: 'I wish my journey may be of use to the place, which if it should, it will be flattering to me. Nature has been truly bountiful and art has done no harm.'

## Tywi Valley

The lower part of the Tywi valley stretches westwards from the early medieval town of Llandeilo to the ancient county town of Carmarthen. Between the two is a landscape of quite extraordinary beauty and history.

The silhouette of Paxton's Tower stands above the remains of the water gardens created for Sir William Paxton of Middleton Hall in the early 19th century. The tower was built in 1815 in honour of Lord Nelson and was used as a banqueting house. It was linked to the main house by a circuitous carriage drive through the gardens.

Standing on a promontory in the middle of the valley is the medieval Dryslwyn Castle, part of a defensive chain running across southern Wales. Another hill has achieved fame as the subject of a poem by John Dyer (1699-1757) who lived at Aberglasne, the site of another important garden. Grongar Hill was written by Dyer in 1726.

*Grass and flowers Quiet treads,*
*On the meads and mountain-heads,*
*Along with pleasure close ally'd*
*Every by each other's side.*
*And often by the murm'ring rill,*
*Hears the thrush, while all is still,*
*Within the groves of Grongar Hill.*

## Narberth

The town is mainly Georgian in appearance, having undergone a period of prosperity at the turn of the 18th century as a market centre serving the local area. In fact, Narberth is an ancient settlement and appears several times in the fabulous tales of the *Mabinogi*, thought to be the written version of the ancient bardic oral tradition. In one of the stories Pwyll, prince of Dyfed, saw the beautiful Rhiannon riding her magnificent white horse at Narberth.

The town is on the border between North and South Pembrokeshire. George Owen, who wrote a 'Description' of Pembrokeshire in 1603, said the 'shire is taken to be divided into two parts, that is to the Englishry and the Welshry . . . The upper part of the shire . . . is inhabited by Welshmen'. To the south, the incoming 'Normans, Flemings and Englishmen . . . utterly ex-pelled the inhabitants thereof and peopled the county themselves'. This division exists to this day and the line of demarcation, or landsker, has changed little. First established by invading Norsemen and re-emphasized by medieval invaders, the landsker still marks the linguistic divide between north and south.

## Kidwelly Tinplate Works

This ancient borough is rightly renowned for its great castle, but Kidwelly has another claim to fame – it was the site of one of the earliest tinplate works in Britain, founded in 1737. As early as the mid 17th century, the Worshipful Company of Pewterers had petitioned Parliament for the 'suppressinge of the excess and abusive making of Crooked Lane ware [tinplate]'. Doubtless, they realized that tinned plate, which could be fashioned into a wide range of goods, was going to present competition to their trade. So it proved to be when, from the early 18th century, tinplate factories began to appear.

The works have been preserved as part of an industrial museum and much of the original and complex method of making tinplate can be traced. The instal-lation of a huge Foden vertical steam engine to drive the hot rolls in 1879 heralded a period of expansion. The Foden engine's flywheel weighs 42 tons. Sheets of steel were heated in furnaces and passed through the rolls several times, being folded over between each pass to improve the malleability of the sheets.

## Llyn y Fan Fach

The rather prosaic literal translation of Llyn y Fan Fach (the small lake on the peak) does not really do justice to the steep glaciated slopes that overlook the lake. The great ice sheets have eroded the land to produce a series of escarpments that fall sharply to the dark, sometimes forbidding, water. It can change its character and appearance in a moment – from being still and quiet a gust of wind blowing down off the high plateau whirls the surface of the water into wild patterns.

Perhaps at such times the long-awaited reappearance of the fair lady of the lake might just occur. She had appeared before and married a local man on condition that he would never strike her three times with iron. Of course, she brought with her untold riches and produced three strong, healthy sons, and they lived together in great bliss. However, the inevitable happened and she returned to the lake, taking all the animals and wealth with her. Her sons remained and became the Physicians of Myddfai. Fiction blends with fact, since Myddfai was, indeed, famed for its physicians. One of their sayings was that water had three qualities: 'It will produce no sickness, no debt and no widowhood.'

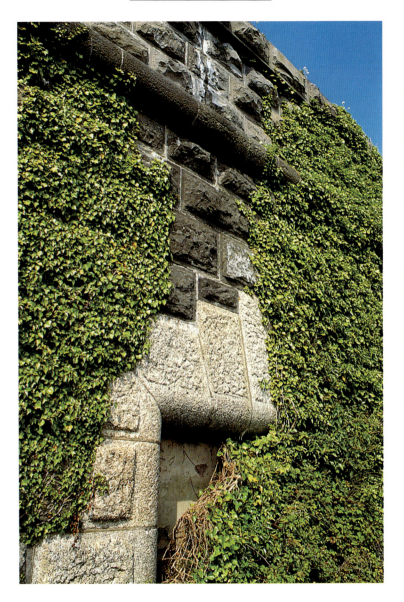

## Milford Haven Fortifications

Admiral Nelson thought Milford Haven one of the finest natural harbours in the world, bettered only by Trincomalee in Ceylon (Sri Lanka). In 1859, a Royal Commission reported on the defence of Britain and considered that the Haven should be fortified to defend the Royal Dockyard that had been established at Pembroke Dock in 1814.

At great expense, massive blockhouse forts were built between 1850 and 1870. They were armed with the latest guns, and heavily defended with granite walls, massive iron doors and shutters. On Stack Rock Fort in the middle of the Haven, the original rifled cannons that fired muzzle-loaded, drop-forged, non-explosive shells thwarted the efforts of the scrap dealers to remove them. One of the guns still lies on the foreshore below Angle Fort.

Altogether, the forts accommodated 1,900 men and 220 heavy guns. But never was a gun fired in anger from any of them. The forts were nicknamed 'Palmerston's Follies' after the prime minister of the day because of the expense, estimated then at £1 million, of their construction.

## Cilgerran Castle

That Cilgerran Castle should have attracted the attentions of J M W Turner and Richard Wilson is not surprising, since the ruins are so romantically placed on top of a well-wooded rocky crag, high above the River Teifi.

The views did not concern the Anglo-Norman builders, who sought to exploit the commanding position over a navigable river as a base to control the hinterland.

The first castle may have been built in 1108 by Gerald of Windsor, who had the site 'fortified with a ditch and wall'. Gerald was married to the beautiful Nest, 'Helen of Wales', and Cilgerran Castle is thought to be the place from where she was abducted by her second cousin, Owain ap Cadwgan. During the mêlée, poor Gerald had to make an undignified escape down one of the latrine shafts.

Cilgerran was a place of attack and counter-attack for centuries, principally between the Welsh and the English, but also with a Viking raid at nearby St Dogmael's Abbey in 1138 for good measure. Slate quarrying in the 19th century caused part of the castle walls to fall with a tremendous crash.

## Aberaeron

The Reverend Benjamin Malkin passed through Aberaeron in 1803 and saw it as 'a poor mud place, but it has on its right a well-wooded, narrow, deep dingle, solitary and picturesque, with a rapid stream running down to the sea'.

Alban Gwynne, a local landowner, saw the potential of the place and promoted a Bill through Parliament to build a new harbour to increase local trade. Rows of houses were laid out in a planned form, initially between 1807 and 1811, followed by further development throughout the century. The houses overlooking the harbour were often the homes of ships' captains and their families.

Much of the town is designated a conservation area and retains an air of restrained Georgian formality, with the brightly painted houses in their precise terraces producing an urban character in the rural surroundings. There is a persistent history that the town was laid out by John Nash. Although there is nothing written to support this supposition, Nash was very active in the area and the town has a great sense of single-mindedness about its design and layout.

## Carew Castle

Sir Rhys ap Thomas was responsible for much of the rebuilding of Carew Castle. He was one of the principal supporters of Henry Tudor, and fought alongside him at Bosworth.

In 1507, Sir Rhys held a great tournament at Carew that lasted for five days and was attended by the aristocracy of Wales, with a small army of retainers. It was reputed that 'although one thousand men had spent five days in company, not one quarrel, unkind word, or cross look had passed between them'.

Sir John Perrot, illegitimate son of Henry VIII, was responsible for the three-storied range with its elegant, mullioned windows overlooking the pool. The upper floor was a long gallery more than 46m (150ft) in length. Gardens and walled courts were built completing the conversion from military stronghold to country residence.

Close to the castle is a Celtic cross, which probably dates from the 10th century.

The last remaining tidal mill in Wales stands on the causeway below the castle. There was a mill on the site in 1558, but the present building dates from the late 18th century.

## Devil's Bridge
*Nr Aberystwyth*

George Borrow was impressed with the bridges that span the narrow chasm formed by the erosive action of the Mynach. The river flows rapidly through the narrow openings, tumbling over a series of small waterfalls.

'The fall, which is split in two, is thundering besides you; foam, foam, foam is flying all about you; the basin or cauldron is boiling frightfully below you; hirsute rocks are frowning terribly above you, and above them forest trees, dank and wet with spray and mist, are distilling drops in showers from their boughs.'

There are three bridges above each other. The lowest dates from the 13th century and still carried traffic until a new one was built in 1753. Both were overshadowed by the bridge of 1901, which has since been altered to carry motor vehicles.

The problems of building the first bridge over the gorge were overcome by the Devil, who struck a bargain that he would build the bridge in return for the soul of the first living thing to cross it. The canny local inhabitants easily outwitted him by rolling a loaf of bread over the bridge, followed by a hungry dog.

## Nanteos
### Nr Aberystwyth

Nanteos (the stream of the night-ingale) is a delightfully emotive name for a house that was once of great importance in the area. It was built in 1737 for Thomas Powell, who had made a fortune out of lead mining in the locality. The exterior is plain and simple, and above a centrally placed portico are three round-headed windows that illuminate an exuberant music room – the showpiece of the house. Large mirrors enlarge the room and increase the feeling of light, and the walls and ceiling are decorated with moulded plasterwork – altogether befitting the cultural and social activity that took place there. Richard Wagner is said to have composed part of *Parsifal* during a stay at Nanteos. George Powell (1842-82) made Nanteos something of a mecca for such artists and writers as Rossetti, Swinburne and Beardsley.

Nanteos is famous for the 'Nanteos Cup' that was once kept there. This is reputedly the Holy Grail used at the Last Supper, which found its way to Nanteos via Glastonbury Abbey. The Cup, made of wood, was imbued with great healing powers and was sought by many visitors. In all probability it was a 15th- or 16th-century drinking bowl.

## St Govan's Chapel
### Nr Pembroke

The Pembrokeshire Coastal Footpath gives access to some of the loveliest coastal scenery in Britain. The stretch around St Govan's Head is breathtaking, with high cliffs that are popular with climbers. Everywhere the sky and cliff ledges are filled with a rich variety of sea birds.

In all weathers these are exciting places, but especially so after a storm, when large waves are still beating against the rocks. Perhaps this is not the time to clamber down the rough steps to St Govan's Chapel, which is wedged in a crack in the cliff face. The present building dates from the 13th century, although the site may have been of monastic importance since the 5th century. No clear identification of St Govan has emerged, but legend says that he was Sir Gwaine, one of King Arthur's knights who entered into a state of retreat in his later years.

Large rocks are scattered outside, and beneath one it is said is a hoard of gold hidden in advance of a Viking attack. When struck the rock will ring like a bell.

The small vaulted building of local limestone is built over a holy well that was reported as having dried in the last century.

## Stackpole
### Nr Pembroke

Between about 1790 and the mid 19th century, the Cawdor family was engaged in a programme of improvement that has resulted in one of the loveliest examples of landscaping in Wales. They saw the potential of flooding the valleys to create a series of freshwater lakes that run down to the sea at Broadhaven. To do so required relocating a village and building a complex system of weirs and watercourses. Special attention was given to the view from the mansion, and the lakes are designed to lead the eye into the distance, broken by an 'eye catcher' bridge.

The lakes are now a haven for wildlife, including otters and monstrous pike. In the last century a pike weighing 14.7kg (32½lb) was caught. The lakes are famous for their lilies, best seen in July and August, and are a National Nature Reserve managed jointly by the Countryside Council for Wales and the National Trust. The lakes are fed by freshwater springs percolating through the limestone. A network of footpaths crosses the estate and links the lakes together.

## Newgale

It is to be expected that Giraldus Cambrensis, the Norman-Welsh chronicler, should think that his native Pembrokeshire 'is the most beautiful . . . the finest part of the province of Demetia'.

Along the length of the coastal path the views are varied, with high cliffs, deeply incised flooded valleys, small coves and many tiny harbours. Everywhere there are sea birds whirling and diving.

One of the best known views is from the main road between Haverfordwest and St David's at Newgale where it drops sharply towards the sea. Beyond, the coast dips and rises, punctuated by many small coves, including Caerbwdi, where the purple-coloured stones for St David's Cathedral were quarried. Further along is Porth Glais, traditionally known as the place where St David was baptized.

When passing over 'Niwgal sands' in 1188, Giraldus Cambrensis referred to a notable event when a great storm exposed the surface of the earth that had been covered for many years and he saw 'trunks of trees cut off, standing in the very sea itself, the strokes of the hatchet appearing as if made yesterday'.

## Llanerchaeron
### Nr Aberaeron

Llanerchaeron is a rare survival of a once typical West Wales estate. The present house, farm buildings and walled gardens were built between 1794 and 1830 and the core of the estate has remained remarkably unchanged.

The main house is notable as the least altered remaining example of John Nash's work in Wales. Commissioned by Colonel William Lewis, Nash applied all his skills as both architect and protagonist of the 'picturesque'.

The estate is complete in every detail, with pleasure walks that pass through beech woodland, alongside a Victorian fernery, into large walled gardens where espaliered fruit trees and box hedges separate the vegetables and fruit. Heated beds produce early fruit and vegetables and grapes are grown in a greenhouse made of concrete and glass.

A complex of farm buildings, with granary, threshing barn, cow sheds and pig sties, surrounds the Bailiff's House. It was built as a model farm and often produced far more than was needed by the family and estate workers.

The estate is now owned by the National Trust and work is under way to repair the buildings.

## Tenby

The name Tenby is derived from Dinbych (a small fortress) and it is thought that Castle Hill, which overlooks the town and harbour, is the site of a Bronze Age fort established around 550 BC.

The harbour was one of the earliest recorded in Wales when, in 1389, Edward III granted the right to levy a local tax, called 'quayage', to pay for its upkeep. The stone castle was built on its prominent position in the late 11th century, but provided little protection against marauding Welsh princes, who attacked and took the castle on several occasions. Continuing raids prompted William de Valence to fortify Tenby with a continuous wall, including towers and gateways.

In 1651, Tenby suffered from a terrible plague epidemic, which killed 400 people out of a total population of 1,000, and sent the town into a prolonged period of decline. When John Wesley visited in 1784, he saw that 'two thirds of the ancient town are either in ruins or vanished away'. Tenby's renaissance came in the late 18th century when it developed into a 'fair and fashionable' bathing resort. The town was virtually rebuilt and the excellent Georgian terraces provide much of its present charm.

## Laugharne

Early in the morning of Sunday, 3 November 1644, Royalist forces defending Laugharne Castle surrendered to Parliamentarian troops after a seven-day siege. During that time, the attackers lost ten men and the defenders 33. When captured, the castle was the home of Sir John Perrot, who had converted the remains of medieval fortifications into a fine mansion with ornamental gardens.

In the 18th and early 19th centuries, the castle grounds were landscaped, new gardens created, parts of the old walls repaired and a new section built.

Dylan Thomas settled permanently in Laugharne in 1949, having lived there between 1938 and 1940. He wrote the short stories that appeared in *Portrait of the Artist as a Young Dog* in the 18th-century gazebo built in the base of one of the castle's towers. Richard Hughes, author of *In Hazard* and *High Wind in Jamaica*, rented the castle from 1934.

The mainly Georgian town, with its clock-towered town hall built in 1746, looks out upon a sweeping expanse of sandy estuary, across Dylan Thomas's 'heron priested shore'.

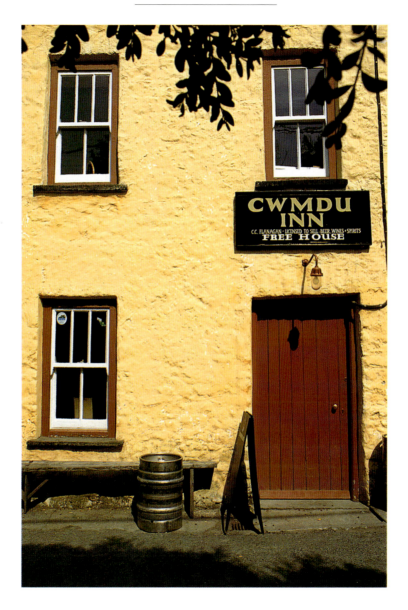

## Cwmdu,
*Nr Llandeilo*

Tucked away in the depths of a lush Carmarthenshire valley, lies the tiny hamlet of Cwmdu. The focal point of the village is a terrace called Rhyd-yr-Onnen (ford of the ash tree). It is flanked by a small chapel and a vestry, which was once the village school. At the end of the terrace is the village inn, originally selling home-brewed beer.

The village shop sold everything the community required. In the 1861 census the owner was described as a 'Master Tailor keeping four hands, grocer, linen and woollen draper and inn keeper'. In his spare time he was a rate collector, band master and secretary of the Oddfellows Benefit Society. A post office was opened in the terrace in 1896.

Such places have mostly disappeared or become so altered as to bear little resemblance to their original appearance and use. Not so with Cwmdu. The hamlet is now owned by the National Trust, which has retained the buildings and their interiors much as they used to be, and the inn, shop and post office are once more open for business. The chapel is still used by its members and the Sunday school in the vestry resounds to the voices of local children.

## Garn Goch
### Nr Llangadog

On the northern edge of the Black Mountain, near Llangadog, are two Iron Age hill forts. The largest, Garn Goch, is the longest in Wales, measuring 640m (2,100ft) along its longitudinal axis. The smaller is minute in comparison, at just over 91m (300ft) in length.

Forts of such size must have been very difficult to defend, with ramparts almost 1.6km (1 mile) in length, although Garn Goch is perfectly located on top of a precipitous slope with the land falling away sharply on one side. In the centre of the fort is a small pond, a very important factor when choosing a site for fortification. It is probable that Garn Goch was a place of refuge to gather women, children and animals while the battles were fought elsewhere.

The fortifications are impressive, with rubble stone walls in places measuring up to 9m (30ft) high, and an entrance lined with large stone slabs.

This is an area of some significant archaeological importance. Nearby, are the remains of a cairn and the site of medieval house platforms.

## Worm's Head
### Rhosili

The Worm's Head is only accessible at low tide across a narrow spit of rocks. At high tide it is surrounded by water and, from the right angle, it does look like a 'wurm', the Old English word for dragon or serpent. At Paviland cave on Gower, the skeleton of a 'Red Lady' was discovered in 1823. It turned out to be a man whose remains had been stained with red ochre. Carbon dating has revealed that he lived about 24,000 years ago.

An ancient field system encloses the tiny village of Rhosili. Known locally as 'The Vile', which means simply 'field' in Old English, low stone walls form the boundaries between strips of land known as landshares. The magnificent beach sweeps in an elongated 5 km (3 mile) curve below Rhosili Down and is broken only by the sparse ribs of the barque *Helvetia* wrecked during a storm in November 1877.

A lonely house in the middle of the expanse of solifluction terrace is a former rectory. It stands a short distance away from the site of a medieval village that was gradually overwhelmed by shifting, drifting sands during the 14th century.

# SOUTH EAST

**Blaenrhondda**

As the demand for coal increased in the last quarter of the 19th century so pits were sunk and communities developed in the small valleys leading off the main Rhondda valleys. At the head of Rhondda Fawr the houses followed the general pattern of development, spreading along the floor of the valley in long straggling lines. Between 1881 and 1914 over 10,000 houses were built in the valleys, most of them of five small rooms, costing about £140 each to build. A Ministry of Health report published in 1920 stated that many 'houses generally have a little-used front parlour with a kitchen behind and a kitchen scullery in the back projection. Families usually live in the two back rooms'.

Nearly three million people live in Wales today, and more than two-thirds of them are to be found in the South East of the country, in an area bounded by Swansea to the west, the border with England to the east and the Brecon Beacons to the north.

During the 18th and 19th centuries, thousands of people flooded into the valleys seeking a better life through employment in the iron works, coal mines and ancillary trades and industries. In the space of a few hundred years the economy of the locality was turned on its head, as dependence on agriculture was replaced by industrialization. This began in the 16th century when charcoal-fuelled iron furnaces were built near ore deposits and, much more importantly, close to plentiful supplies of timber, and water to drive waterwheels.

In the 19th century, the valleys to the north of Cardiff were transformed as coke instead of charcoal was used to smelt iron. In addition, after 1875 the British Admiralty decided that Welsh steam coal was the best fuel for their warships. This was the land where 'King Coal' reigned supreme. His subjects worked in seams of 'black gold' and the rush for coal changed the environment dramatically. Into the iron towns and mining valleys poured thousands of people from all parts of Britain and sometimes further afield; a street in Dowlais is named 'Alphonso Row' following its early immigrants from Spain. The valleys at that time were places of political, religious and social ferment. Chapels serving the Nonconformist cause were built at a rate of one every week, and the politics moved from liberalism to socialism. Parts of Rhondda, for example, were nicknamed 'Little Moscow'.

South Wales produced more than its fair share of musicians, and many chapels were large enough and had sufficient singers to put on complete performances of *The Messiah* and *Elijah*. Joseph Parry, born in May 1841 in a tiny, canal-side cottage in Merthyr Tydfil, became one of the best known composers of his day. His song *Myfanwy* is almost compulsory for inclusion in any self-respecting male-voice choir's repertoire. Cilfynydd, consisting of little more than half a dozen terraces above Pontypridd, produced Sir Geraint Evans and Stuart Burrows.

Westwards, Swansea, the 'ugly, lovely' birthplace of Dylan Thomas, looks across a long, curving bay towards Mumbles. An area of the town in the late 18th century was

## Tabernacle Chapel
*Morriston*

The only census of religious accommodation in Britain was taken in 1851 and revealed that the building of chapels was far outstripping that of churches. During the 19th century, more than 5,000 chapels were built in Wales; between 1800 and 1850 they were being built at a rate of one every eight days. In the burgeoning industrial communities, they became not only places of worship but also centres of education and recreation. Strangers arriving in a town would head for the chapel of 'their' denomination, where they would be guaranteed a welcome.

As the 19th century progressed so the chapels became larger and increasingly ornate. No longer did they reflect the local vernacular architecture but rather drew their inspiration from the ancient and classical orders.

Described as the 'Cathedral of Nonconformity', Tabernacle Chapel in Morriston is the apogee of chapel building, costing £18,000 to build in 1872. The design was copied many times. The focal point is the pulpit, below which is the Sedd Fawr (big seat) for the deacons.

The inscription translates as *Worship the Lord in the Beauty of Holiness.*

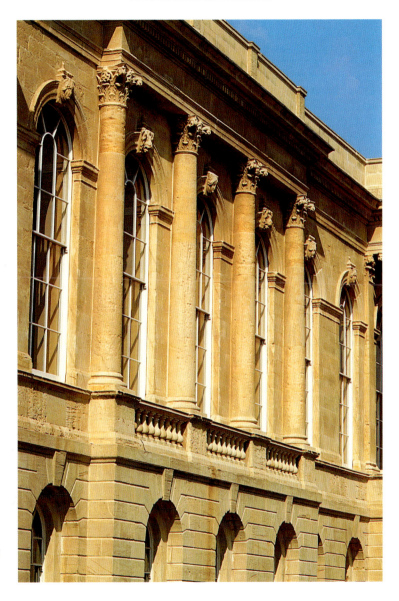

## Swansea

Swansea is the second largest town in Wales with a history spanning more than a thousand years. Its name is thought to derive from a Norse chieftain, Sweyn Forkbeard, who established a camp on one of the small islands – an 'ey', hence Sweyn's ey.

Swansea grew in importance during the 18th and 19th centuries as industry developed, earning it the nickname 'Copperopolis' from the concentration of copper smelters. The town has long prided itself on its cultural activities – the first newspaper in Wales, the *Cambrian*, was published in the town in 1804, followed by the Welsh language *Seren Gomer* in 1815.

Large docks were built and the course of the River Tawe was altered. The docklands became the main centre of commerce and many fine houses and grand public buildings were built. The Guildhall was opened in 1847 and served the town for many years. Swansea suffered severe bombing during World War II and the docks declined as the old industries closed. Over the past decade there has been a revival in the fortunes of the area. The Guildhall is now the National Literature Centre for Wales.

## Llandrindod Wells

Perhaps it is not surprising that the Romans established a camp at Castell Collen, near what was to become Llandrindod Wells. They probably knew of the saline springs and those containing chalybeate and sulphur that were to give the town notoriety in the 18th century and respectability in the 19th.

The springs were rediscovered by a Mrs Jenkins in 1736 and she reported that cures had been effected by their use. The first hotel was built by Mr Grosvenor in 1749 and from then until its closure in 1787 it was, as Lewis's *Topographical Dictionary* stated, the 'rendez-vous chiefly for fashionable gamesters and libertines'.

With the coming of the railway in 1865 the character of the town changed. New hotels were built and the small vernacular dwellings were replaced by large, elegant town houses suitable for the 80,000 visitors who came to take the waters every year.

The town has some of the very best examples of Victorian and Edwardian architecture in Wales, and to visit during 'Victorian Week', when everybody dresses in authentic costume, is to experience a feeling of time travel.

## Blacksmith, Penybont
*Nr Llandrindod Wells*

The Price family moved to the smithy at Penybont in 1900, and fires have burned in the forge ever since. It is a rare survival of the days of horse transport and the present blacksmith remembers when there would be 'four or six horses waiting outside' to be shod. The charges were 8 shillings for a pony and 10 shillings for a cart horse and, as a special service, the cost of 'taking off the four shoes, cutting his feet down and renailing the shoes' was one shilling.

The shutters were used for testing the brands that were specially made for the local farms. No two brands were ever the same, so the shutters also served as a record. Care was required to ensure that the actual symbol was not made too deep, otherwise application of the hot irons could cause even greater distress to the animal.

Like other smithies, the Price family were called on to repair tools and equipment and they made more than 30 different types of bill hook to suit all the purposes of the locality. They also sold Swedish pitch, used to cauterize the snicks caused when shearing sheep, and also for sealing coffins.

## Mynydd Eppynt

This is one of the last 'wilderness' areas of Wales – due mainly to the presence of the army who use large areas as a firing range and training ground. The families who had lived here for generations were moved out during World War II.

It is a land of high, undulating moorlands, incised by steep valleys and rapid streams. The area is crisscrossed with a network of trackways, many abandoned. Few roads traverse the range, but one follows the route of a drover's road, one of the main routes towards England. Drovers were vital to the economy of rural West Wales. The cattle raised in the sparse uplands were described as 'razor-backed mongrels' so their slow, careful movement eastwards was geared around the availability of good grazing.

A local historian mused on the movement of these great herds: 'It must have been a grand sight, the massive jet beasts leisurely labouring upwards with here and there in view a single horseman in charge, and then would come the thought that none of these thousands of cattle would ever return.'

## Baptist Chapel
*Capel-y-Ffin*

The hamlet of Capel-y-Ffin (chapel of the boundary) lies in the depths of the beautiful Vale of Ewyas, between Abergavenny and Hay-on-Wye. It takes its name from the church that was built in 1762 on the site of an earlier place of worship. A short distance below the church is a small, whitewashed Baptist chapel, established by the efforts of two pious brothers – William and David Prosser. A wall plaque commemorates their work in bringing 'The Ministry of the Gospel, to their house in the year 1737. And Secured this Place for That Sacred Use for the Time Being. Both died near the End of the Year 1780.'

The tiny church and chapel stand in contrast to the magnificent Llanthony Abbey further down the valley. Giraldus Cambrensis visited the abbey while fund raising for the third crusade in 1188 and noted: 'The monks gaze up at the distant prospects which rise above their own lofty roof-tops, and there they see, as far as any eye can reach, mountain peaks which rise to meet the sky and often enough herds of wild deer which are grazing on their summits.'

## Maesyronnen Chapel
*Nr Glasbury*

The Act of Uniformity was entered in the statute books on 19 April 1662 and saw the lawful division between the Dissenters and the established Church, albeit treatment of those who refused to 'conform' could still be harsh. It was not until 1669, when the 'Toleration Act' was passed, that pressure began to ease although 'nonconformists' were treated with suspicion for many years.

The early Nonconformists held their meetings in secret, afraid of persecution, using remote farmhouses and barns as places of worship. After the passing of the Act they began converting existing buildings and erecting new chapels. Many of the early places of worship have been enlarged and altered. Maesyronnen, near Glasbury, is one of the few places that has remained unchanged and its interior is a reminder of the simplicity of the early years of the movement. Its layout was the standard that was adopted for the thousands of chapels that were built in the following centuries.

Maesyronnen Chapel was formerly a barn attached to an Elizabethan house and was converted to a chapel in 1696. Part of the building is now a Landmark Trust property.

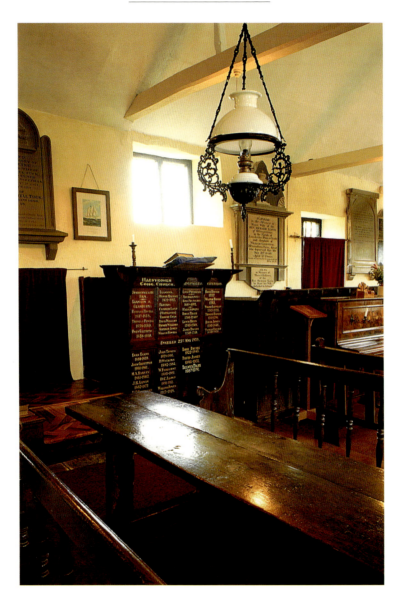

## Pontneddfechan Powder Works

*The Cambrian* newspaper of 10 April 1857 reported that: 'last week we mentioned that the Walet Falls of the upper part of the Vale of Neath were likely to be made the site of a gunpowder manufactory. The promoters of the undertaking obtained at the Breconshire Quarter Sessions on Wednesday last a licence to erect their mills over a space of two miles including the Upper and Lower Cilliepste Falls.'

The mills were duly built alongside the river by 1863 and a series of buildings related to the various manufacturing processes were linked by a horse-drawn tramroad. The horse shoes were made of brass to avoid sparks.

The main output of the works was explosives for the coal-mining industry, and as that industry declined so, too, did powder production. The works closed in 1939.

Power was provided by water drawn from the river and conducted via watercourses to drive the turbines. Today, the site has been long abandoned and the ruins of the buildings are set in the most delightful of surroundings, hidden in woodland that reaches to the edge of the river.

### Blorenge
*Nr Abergavenny*

Between Abergavenny and Blaenafon is a landscape rich in the remains of the industrial revolution of South East Wales. The *Universal British Directory* of 1791 stated that the 'mountains in this neighbourhood abound with ore, coal and lime'. Arch-deacon Coxe visited Blaenafon in 1801 and recorded that at 'some distance the works have the appearance of a small town sur-rounded with heaps of ore, coal and limestone and enlivenment with all the bustle and activity of an opulent and increasing estab-lishment'.

This is the landscape that inspired Alexander Cordell to write his bestseller *Rape of the Fair Country*. In the late 18th and 19th centuries this was an area of great industrial importance, with a network of tramroads and water-courses crisscrossing the hillsides, linking the works and quarries and connecting to the Brecon and Abergavenny Canal.

The old industries have finished producing marketable products but they still have an important function as tourist attractions.

The former tramroads make excellent footpaths in this terrain, carefully following the contours before plunging down the incline to the canal on the valley floor.

### Scwd Eira
*Vale of Neath*

A visitor to Scwd Eira (the falls of snow) in 1813 wrote that the water 'precipitates itself with such force as to leave a considerable space between the perpendicular rock and the part beneath; this aqueous arch is a common path for men and cattle, who find a nearer cut by this extraordinary road to the neighbouring villages.' This is one of a series of water-falls on the tributaries that feed the River Neath. The rivers are hidden in deep, narrow, wooded valleys that intersect the open moorland above. The trees meet overhead to form green tunnels through which rivers tumble and fall with ferocity.

In very wet weather, Scwd Eira forms a graceful curve as a series of falls combine to produce a small-scale Niagara. The water flows over a lip of sandstone on the top of a band of soft shale that has been eroded to such an extent it is possible to walk behind the sheet of water. At the base of the falls, a deep pool has been formed by the constant movement of loose stones.

## Clytha Castle
*Nr Raglan*

Clytha Castle stands in a prominent position high above and visible from Clytha Court, a delightful Greek revival house of 1824. Clytha Court was designed by Edward Haycock, a pupil of Jeffrey Wyatville, and the castle has been attributed to John Nash. The owner of the house, William Jones, was responsible for the construction of the nearby sham castle. This was built in 1790 and carries an inscription stating that it was 'undertaken for the purposes of relieving a mind sincerely afflicted by the loss of a most excellent wife whose remains were deposited in Llanarth Churchyard AD 1787 and to the memory of whose virtues this tablet is dedicated'. The lady in question, Elizabeth, also has a memorial in the local church.

The castle is owned by the National Trust with part of it leased to the Landmark Trust. The left-hand tower is roofless, and was only ever designed to be a shell, to lend symmetry to the façade. The surrounding land is owned by the National Trust and tenanted; a footpath links with Coed-y-Bwnydd, an Iron Age fort about 1.6km (1 mile) away.

Llangorse Lake

The lake stretches over 2.5km (1½ miles) and is the largest area of natural water in South Wales. In the 19th century there was great excitement in archaeological circles with the discovery of lake dwellings on the continent and in Ireland and Scotland. In 1925 there was a remarkable discovery of a virtually complete dug-out boat at Llangorse, and carbon dating indicates a 9th-century origin.

This fits the research that has unfolded a fascinating story about the crannog, an artificial island a short distance from the shore. It is similar to lake dwellings elsewhere, constructed of massive planks of oak behind which the dwelling platform was formed of layers of stone, soil and brushwood. Much of its history has been revealed by archaeologists, but a reference in the Anglo-Saxon Chronicle has shed new light. In 916 'Aethelflaed sent an army into Wales and destroyed Brecenanmere and captured the king's wife and 33 other persons'. The crannog at Llangorse was a Royal residence of the King of Brycheiniog at the time.

## Dyffryn House and Gardens
### Nr Cardiff

Whereas the early 19th-century ironmasters tended to live close to their great works, the 'Kings of Coal' later in the century built large houses away from the coal-fields that generated their wealth.

Dyffryn House is a typical example. Built by John Cory in 1893, it replaced an 18th-century house owned by another coal magnate, Thomas Pryce. In contrast to the environment of the mining valleys, Dyffryn Gardens is a series of garden 'rooms'.

Each room is enclosed within hedges and boundaries, including the oldest – the kitchen and rose garden – that has its origins in the 16th century. After John Cory's death in 1910, the garden was taken over by his son Reginald, one-time vice president of the Royal Horticultural Society. He sponsored plant collecting expeditions to many parts of the world and the results of his endeavours are to be seen today at Dyffryn. He engaged architect Thomas Mawson to redesign the gardens, and a tour of Italy provided the inspiration for the Pompeiian garden enclosed within its arcades of pillars. This was just one of the rooms where both he and his client 'felt at liberty to indulge in every phase of garden design . . .'.

## Kenfig Dunes
### Nr Port Talbot

The National Nature Reserve at Kenfig is a haven of wildlife and natural landscape. Although it is close to the sea, in the centre of the dune complex is a 70-acre freshwater pool that provides a habitat for many species of wild-fowl. Legend supposes Kenfig to be the site of a medieval town that was submerged by a great storm in the 14th century. On stormy nights, the bells of the church are said to ring a muffled toll beneath the waters. Richard Fenton visited Kenfig in 1803 and described it as: '. . . a lake of some extent, in the midst of naked sands. It is said never to have been fathomed. Here also we are told of a town ingulphed; and they go so far as to say that at times the tops of the buildings may be seen: but this is rather too much.'

Like so many legends, there is some fact behind the stories. The remains of a small, stone castle are visible and a medieval town did exist and was gradually over-whelmed by shifting sands and ultimately abandoned. The land is owned by the trustees of the Kenfig Corporation, who are the modern-day successors to the medieval burgesses of the ancient borough.

## The Common,
### *Pontypridd*

The circles and spirals of stones, some with mystical carvings, are the result of the imagination and beliefs of a 19th-century eccentric. Dr William Price was a famous figure in South Wales, especially after the trial in 1884 when he was accused of illegally cremating his son, Iesu Grist. He represented himself at the trial and won, thus establishing the legality of cremation. He did not believe in marriage, considering it a form of bondage, advocated free love and fathered a child when he was 90 years old.

In addition to being a physician and amateur lawyer, he was also an ardent Chartist, and his involvement in the cause of the 1830s necessitated his flight to Paris disguised as a woman.

Pontypridd is located at the entrance to the Rhondda and Merthyr and Aberdare Valleys. It, therefore, became the meeting place for the valleys and developed into an important town towards the end of the 19th century. The Rocking Stone (a geological curiosity – the stone once could be rocked by a person standing on top of it) became the meeting point for those involved in coal-mining strikes. In 1893 it was estimated that over 20,000 people gathered during the first national strike of miners.

## Llanhilleth Workingmen's Institute

In the industrial valleys of South Wales few buildings stand above the serried ranks of stone-and-slate cottages that snake their way across and along the contours. The exceptions are the chapels and workingmen's institutes, both places representing aspects of life in the valleys.

The institutes were built in response to the demands of the workingmen and their families for places of entertainment and education. Subscriptions were raised and building work was financed by bazaars and concerts. Running costs were covered by income generated in the halls themselves and by voluntary deductions from miners' wages.

Few of these buildings remain and those that do are finding it difficult to survive in these days of sophisticated entertainment. Llanhilleth is the exception. Opened on the 12 May 1905, at a cost of £3,000, its façade was altered in the 1920s to accommodate cinema projectors.

An architect engaged to design one of the institutes was given the instruction by the management committee about the size of building and the type of facilities required, but with the stipulation that it should be designed 'in the renaissance manner'.

## Ewenni Priory
*Nr Bridgend*

When the antiquarian Benjamin Malkin visited Ewenni Priory in 1803 he took on the mantle of a latter-day conservationist by discovering the 'most perfect specimen of a monastic establishment' and noting that 'the proprietor, who should have been better advised on the subject, was beginning to pull some part of it to pieces, for the purpose of modernising a residence for himself'.

Maurice de Londres, the first Norman Lord of Ogmore, gave land to monks from Gloucester Cathedral in c. 1120 to build a Benedictine priory on the site of an earlier church. Ewenni Priory is one of the best examples of relatively untouched Norman architecture extant and displays an uncompromising attitude in its design. Massive drum pillars support the vaulted roof in the earlier northern section, and on these pillars there are faint images of saints. The eastern section of the church is impressively simple. An arcade of round-headed arches illuminates a narrow passage giving access to the bell tower. After the Dissolution the monastic buildings, other than the nave that remained the parish church, were granted to the local family.

## Brecon Beacons

The escarpments of Pen y Fan and Corn Du are in great contrast with the wider area known as the Brecon Beacons. The old red sandstone that forms the bulk of the range has been moulded and weathered into undulating hills with small, tree-filled valleys. At Pen y Fan the open plateau suddenly plunges, sliced away by the erosive action of glaciation.

These mountains are not always as benign as they look. Corn Du, at 873m (2,863ft), can experience weather changes in a matter of minutes, from bright sunlight at one moment to cold clammy mists the next. The Brecon Beacons are of great significance to the people of the industrialized areas a short distance to the south. Every day of the year there will be someone walking the footpaths, and there is a constant battle to keep the trails repaired and accessible. On the higher slopes can be found some of the most southerly alpine-like plants in Britain.

The *Gossiping Guide to Wales* (1895) confidently declared that the view: '. . . extends to the Bristol Channel and the coast of Somersetshire, Swansea Bay, and, we believe, the lighthouse on the Mumbles; north-west to Plynlimon and Cadair Idris.'

## Gnoll Estate Cascades
*Neath*

Christies of London sold the Gnoll Estate in 1801 and their sale catalogue gave these details: 'Gnoll Estate is diversified with hill, dale, wood and water in the most sublime and enchanting style, and environed by vast amphitheatres of hills and broken woody ground intercepting a view of the sea and watered by numerous fine streams.' No mention is made of the smoke and fumes from the copperworks and coal mines that surrounded the house for miles around and produced the wealth for the family to live in such style.

The cascade had been introduced as an 'improvement' to the estate and took advantage of a steep slope to allow water to tumble down a series of falls and small pools. One of the tourists of the time, the Hon John Byng, visited in 1787 and was impressed by the 'fall of water 300 feet over great rocks, towards a root house, where we sat: and saw the reservoir let loose to roll the stream with great vehemence'.

Gnoll House was demolished in 1957 but its gardens survived and are being preserved. At the head of the cascade are the twin towers of a castellated folly, below which is a grotto complete with artificial stalagmites.

## Round Houses
*Nant-y-glo*

A huge gulf existed between the early 19th-century ironmasters and their families and the people employed in their ironworks, mines and quarries. The first three decades of the century represented a time of political and social ferment, with strikes and riots against poor conditions and low wages. At Nant-y-glo (stream of coal) in Monmouthshire, the ironmaster was concerned enough to build two fortified towers to guard a farm and storage building, and as a place of refuge for himself and his family.

Nant-y-glo was one of the places where 'Scotch Cattle' were very active. This was a secret underground movement that punished those they regarded as betraying their cause, offending against morality or exploiting the people. Houses were visited at night by groups up to 200 strong and usually the windows were broken. In extreme cases, the house was wrecked and the men beaten.

The towers were small fortresses, entirely fireproof, with the roof, doors and windows made of iron. The windows were shuttered and the main door on one of the towers has musket apertures set low down so the shots could be aimed at the knees of attackers. Happily the towers were never attacked.

## Porth yr Ogof

The great South Wales coalfield is bordered by a rim of carboniferous limestone. The rock is water soluble and traversed by many joints and fissures. Water percolating through the vertical and horizontal joints has widened and eroded them, forming an important cave system between the head of the Swansea valley and just below Abergavenny.

Porth yr Ogof is one of the best-known caves, particularly because of its massive entrance formed where the River Mellte runs into the cave from a narrow gorge. It has been popular with visitors for more than 200 years. William Young in his *Guide to the Scenery of Glyn Neath*, published in 1835, recommended a visit because: '. . . this is a remarkable object; for although openings or caves in the limestone rock abound in this vicinity, there is not another in the valley of so large dimensions; you have light enough from the entrance to go in a considerable distance.'

Some of the caves in the area have been surveyed and the largest, Ogof Ffynnon Ddu (the cave of the black spring) has accessible passages more than 45km (28 miles) long.

## Grosmont

In the borderland between Wales and England it is perhaps not surprising to find a place name that is derived neither from Welsh nor English, but is Norman in origin. On top of Grosmont (big hill) stands a castle that, with two others at Skenfrith and White Castle, forms a triangle. Together they were part of the lines of protection along the borderlands. Grosmont Castle was attacked by Owain Glyn Dŵr in 1405; in the 16th century it was described as being in decay.

Grosmont is now a small village but it was once a medieval township of some importance. It was granted a borough charter, possibly as early as 1219, and by 1250 there may have been as many as 160 burgage plots. Corporation status was retained until 1857, when it still had a mayor and an official ale taster.

The present town hall dates from 1832 and replaces a timber structure, a market was held in the town twice a week. The 14th-century church was restored by J P Seddon in 1869 and in its nave is a large effigy of a knight referred to locally as Jack O' Kent, who was a 'worker of wonders' and a wizard.

## Brecon and Abergavenny Canal

The Brecon and Abergavenny Canal runs through lovely countryside deep into the Brecon Beacons National Park and formed an important link between the industrial communities and the rural hinterland. The canal was opened along its full length between Pontypool, where it joins with the Monmouthshire Canal, and the market town of Brecon in 1812.

For the most part, the canal follows the natural contours, with just six locks along its length of 53km (33 miles). Just beyond bridge 114 the canal crosses over a small aqueduct, one of many. Until 1970 the through route to Brecon was blocked by a low, fixed bridge, which was replaced by a drawbridge. The canal is now very popular with leisure craft, in contrast to its origins as a thoroughfare for narrow boats carrying manufacturing and mining products. The link with Brecon was very important, since foodstuffs from the rural area were vital for the expanding industrial towns. Because of the topography, the canals of South Wales depended on a network of tramroads to connect with the factories. Another important cargo was lime, and the remains of many lime kilns are found at intervals alongside the 'cut'.

## Cardiff Castle

In 1801 the population of Cardiff was about 1,800. By 1901 it had rocketed to 164,330, becoming the largest town in Wales and its most important commercial and business centre. The opening of West Bute Dock in 1839 had given added impetus to the development of the port after the opening of the Glamorgan Canal from Merthyr Tydfil in 1794. The Taff Vale Railway into the Rhondda and Taff Valleys followed, and further expansion of the docks saw Cardiff become the largest and most important coal-exporting port in Britain.

It was the 3rd Marquess of Bute, fabulously rich from the proceeds of industrialization, who created one of the masterpieces of Victorian medieval fantasy. In 1868 the Marquess, with his architect William Burgess, began work on enlarging Cardiff Castle and transforming it into an architectural extravaganza. Burgess and the Marquess let their imaginations run riot. Everywhere are highly decorated surfaces, gilded and painted, and expanses of tiled floors, inlaid wood and metals. Inside the walls is a surprise – one of the best-preserved examples of a Norman motte and keep in Wales. Nearby Bute Park, which extends from the Castle towards Llandaff Cathedral, was presented by the Marquess of Bute to the city in 1947.

## Gwent Levels

The unprepossessing name of Gwent Levels belies an area of great beauty and important archaeological content. In the Severn Estuary, between the mouths of the rivers Wye and Usk, is an area of flat land known as the Levels – a large expanse of reclaimed land protected by a sea wall and drained by ditches.

A remarkable discovery in 1986 provided a very human link with the distant past. Heavy storms and tides revealed a series of footprints left in mud during the mesolithic period. Detailed excavation and research has revealed that one of the lines of prints was probably made by a man of average size walking carefully across the treacherous mud flats. Traces of Iron Age trackways and houses have also been discovered.

The proximity of the Levels to large conurbations has placed pressure on the area, with new roads and development ever present. The ecology of the Levels is delicately poised, with its freshwater wetlands providing habitats for a wide range of bird and animal life. Many areas are designated Sites of Special Scientific Interest.

## Tredegar House
### Nr Newport

Tredegar House, near Newport, is among the finest examples of 17th-century houses in Britain. Between 1664 and 1672 the house was rebuilt, replacing a house that was in existence in 1402. It was owned by Llywelyn ap Morgan, but he had forfeited his estates as punishment for supporting Owain Glyn Dŵr.

The Morgan family lived in the house from the early years of the 15th century and remained in occupation until 1951. In the 1930s and 1940s Tredegar House was known for the parties given by Evan, Viscount Tredegar. He was often accompanied by his pet parrot, Blue Boy, perched on his shoulder. Among the guests were H G Wells and Prince Paul of Greece, who would have been amused by the menagerie of animals in the grounds, including a boxing kangaroo.

The house was used a girls' school until the early 1970s, but on being taken over by the local authority it was found to be suffering from both dry and wet rot. Since that time, the property has undergone a remarkable transformation: the fine interiors have now been restored and the exterior and the grounds have been repaired and returned to their former high standard.

## Cefn Golau
### Nr Tredegar

On a windswept mountain top between Rhymni and Tredegar in Monmouthshire is a melancholy reminder of the social conditions in the 19th-century 'iron towns'. It is a graveyard, long abandoned and unloved, but important as one of the few cholera burial grounds extant in Wales.

The first recorded death from cholera was in Sunderland in 1831, and at intervals throughout the century the disease struck many parts of Britain. At the time, the reasons for the disease were not understood, and it was referred to as 'God's Awful Fear' and the 'Great Miasma'. It was often caused by pollution of water supplies, not an unusual occurrence in the 19th century.

At Cefn Golau (ridges of light) the gravestones bear sombre witness to the rapidity of death after onset of the disease. One of the inscriptions is to the memory of Thomas James who died on 18 August 1849, aged 20 years, and it reads:

*One night and day I bore great pain*
*To try for cure was all in vain*
*But God knew what to me was best,*
*Did ease my pain and give me rest.*

## Merthyr Tydfil

Merthyr Tydfil was described as a 'miserable straggling village' in the 1760s. By 1860, it was the principal town of Wales and the 'iron making capital of the world'.

The first iron furnace was in blast in 1765 and the next hundred years saw the creation of a totally industrial landscape. Poor sanitation and polluted water supplies created appalling conditions. The average life expectancy of a working person in the mid 19th century was about 17 years. A police sergeant stated: 'The overcrowding is excessive, in one small room there are five beds. The roof or ceiling is so low that in one case there is not room to sit up in bed. There is no drainage whatever, and no privy; nor, indeed, the right to the use of a privy to any of these houses.'

The town is composed of a series of communities that grew up around the various ironworks. The Dowlais Iron Company was the largest and the owner, John Guest, had the Dowlais Stables built in 1820 for the company horses. The rooms on the top floor were used as a school, for which children were charged a penny or twopence a week, depending on what the family could afford.

## Tintern and the Wye Valley

The Wye valley inspired Reverend William Gilpin, but of Tintern Abbey he wrote: 'Though parts are beautiful, the whole is ill-shaped.' He recommended that to make it more picturesque a 'mallet judiciously used might be of service in fracturing some of them [the walls], particularly those of the cross isles, which are not only disagreeable in themselves, but confound the perspective'.

Thankfully his specifications did not prevail. Quite the reverse, since much time and trouble has been taken by Cadw to retain the beauty and magnificence of the Abbey. It was founded in 1131 by the Cistercian order and was substantially rebuilt at the end of the 13th century. At the Dissolution, it was the richest Abbey in Wales.

The Abbey and its setting provided an inspiration for its 'romantic' visitors. William Wordsworth revisited on 13 July 1798 and wrote one of the best-known romantic poems, which begins:

*Five years have past; five
    summers, with the length
Of five long winters! and again I
    hear
Those waters, rolling from their
    mountain-springs
With a soft inland murmur*

## Penyclawdd Court

Penyclawdd Court is one of the ancient houses of Wales and has been carefully and lovingly restored. There has been a settlement at Penyclawdd for over 1,000 years, since the Dark Ages, and adjacent to the house are the remains of a motte and bailey built by the Normans. In 1349, Penyclawdd was granted manorial status 'held by half a Knight's Fee by Walter de Kymbard from Lawrence de Hastings'. The present house dates from about 1500, with alterations and additions right through to the Victorian period.

Careful research and study of the house itself have revealed that the parlour wing was built in 1617 from the proceeds of a legacy of silver plate. Bradney's *History of Monmouthshire*, 1906, records Penyclawdd as having been 'a roomy mansion [with] remains of walls enclosing gardens but the whole had become sadly neglected'.

The house is a maze of rooms set at different levels, with low – sometimes very low – ceilings. Everywhere is a wealth of architectural and archaeological detail. The dining room has been purposely kept free of electricity so meals are taken by candlelight and the glow of logs burning in the large inglenook.

## Rhondda

Rhondda was once synonymous with coal mining. The first pits were opened in the 18th century and over the next hundred years the population of the valleys leapt as more collieries opened. In the 1870s, the rate of development accelerated until, by 1924, more than 160,000 people were crammed into the narrow valleys. Life was dominated by the pit-head hooter sounding the changes of shifts or the heart-stopping signals that heralded an accident.

Lewis Jones, born in 1897 in Clydach Vale, wrote: 'The wind howled over the mountains and swept down . . . as though chased by a million nightmares . . . A tall smokestack stuck its head through the ruddy glow of the pit furnaces, too proud to notice the clamour of the storm, above which sounded the "chug-chug" of the pit engines, broken at short intervals by a "clanketty-clang" as the pit spewed two trams full of coal into the storm and sucked two empties out of it.'

History has turned full circle and all the collieries in Rhondda have closed. Most of their traces have been swept away except for the Lewis Merthyr Colliery in Trehafod, which is now the Rhondda Heritage Park.

## The Kymin
*Monmouth*

> *Delightful scene of varied beauty fair!*
> *What eye can o'er thy mingled prospect gaze,*
> *Without a silent, meditative pause*

The Kymin, an anglicization of Cae maen (field of stones), overlooks Monmouth and has superb views in all directions. In the last decades of the 18th century, during 'the most pleasant part of the Summer season, the principal Gentlemen of Monmouth and its vicinity, hold a weekly meeting at the Kymin, on a Tuesday, for the purpose of dining together, and spending the day in a social and friendly manner'. The gentlemen decided to finance 'a slight building erected as a security from the inclemency of the weather' and collected 80 guineas in subscriptions to construct the banqueting house, completed in 1796.

Victory over the French at the Battle of the Nile in 1798 spurred the gentlemen and 'other inhabitants of Monmouth' to subscribe towards the construction of a naval temple, which was opened in 1801. The following year, Lord Nelson, accompanied by Sir William and Lady Emma Hamilton, visited the Kymin and declared it one of the most beautiful places he had ever seen.

# Selected Properties And Regional Offices

**CADW, WELSH HISTORIC MONUMENTS**

**Cadw (Welsh Historic Monuments)**
Crown Building
Cathays Park
Cardiff
CF1 3NQ
Tel: 01222 500 200

**Beaumaris Castle**
Beaumaris
Anglesey LL58 8AP
Tel: 01248 810 361

**Bishops Palace**
St David's
Pembrokeshire SA62 6PE
Tel: 01437 720 517

**Blaenafon Ironworks**
North Street
Blaenafon
Torfaen
Tel: 01495 792 615 *(Summer only)*

**Cilgerran Castle**
Castle House
Cilgerran
Pembrokeshire SA43 2SF
Tel: 01239 615 007

**Conwy Castle**
Conwy
LL32 8LD
Tel: 01492 592 358

**Denbigh Castle**
Castle Hill
Denbigh
Denbighshire LL16 3NB

**Harlech Castle**
Castle Square
Harlech
Gwynedd LL46 2YH
Tel: 01766 780 552

**Laugharne Castle**
King Street
Laugharne
Carmarthenshire
Tel: 01994 427 906 *(Summer only)*

**Rhuddlan Castle**
Rhuddlan
Denbighshire LL18 5AD
Tel: 01745 590 777

**Rhug Chapel**
c\o Coronation Cottage
Rhug
Nr Corwen
Denbighshire LL21 9BT
Tel: 01490 412 025 *(Summer only)*

**Tintern Abbey**
Tintern
Monmouthshire NP6 6SE
Tel: 01291 689 251

**Valle Crucis Abbey**
Llangollen
Denbighshire LL20 8DD
Tel: 01978 860 326 *(Summer only)*

**NATIONAL TRUST**

**Bodnant Garden**
Tal-y-Cafn
Colwyn Bay LL28 5RE
Tel: 01492 650 460

**Chirk Castle**
Chirk
Wrexham LL14 5AF
Tel: 01691 777 701

**Conwy Suspension Bridge**
Conwy
LL32 8LD
Tel: 01492 5732 82

**Cwmdu Inn and Village Shop**
near Llandeilo
Carmarthenshire SA19 7DY
Tel: 01558 685 088

**Dinefwr Park**
Llandeilo
Carmarthenshire SA19 6RT
Tel: 01558 823 092

**Dolau Cothi Gold Mines**
Pumsaint
Carmarthenshire SA19 8RR
Tel: 01558 650 359

**Erddig**
near Wrexham
LL13 0YT
Tel: 01978 355 314

**Llanerchaeron**
near Aberaeron
Ceredigion SA48 8DG
Tel: 01545 570 200

**North Wales Regional Office**
Trinity Square
Llandudno
Gwynedd LL30 2DE
Tel: 01492 860 123

**Penrhyn Castle**
near Bangor
Gwynedd
LL57 4HN
Tel: 01248 353 084

**Plas Newydd**
Llanfairpwll
Anglesey LL61 6DQ
Tel: 01248 714 795

**Powis Castle**
Welshpool
Powys  SY21 8RF
Tel: 01978 554 338

**South Wales Regional Office**
The King's Head
Bridge Street
Llandeilo
Carmarthenshire SA19 6BB
Tel: 01558 822 800

**Ty Mawr Wybrnant**
Penmachno
Betws-y-Coad LL25 0HT
Tel: 01690 760 213

**Tudor Merchant's House**
Quay Hill
Tenby
Pembrokeshire SA70 7BX
Tel: 01834 842 279

**MISCELLANEOUS**

**Big Pit**
Blaenafon
Torfaen NP4 9XP
Tel: 01495 790 311

**Cardiff Castle**
Castle Street
Cardiff CF1 2RB
Tel: 01222 878 100

**Carew Castle**
Carew
Pembrokeshire SA70 8SL
Tel: 01646 651 782

**Devil's Bridge Waterfalls**
Devil's Bridge
near Aberystwyth
Cardiganshire SY23 2JW
Tel: 01970 890 233

**Dyffryn Gardens**
St Nicholas
near Cardiff CF5 6SU
Tel: 01222 593 328

**Ffestiniog Railway**
Harbour Station
Porthmadog
Gwynedd LL49 9NF
Tel: 01766 512 340

**Kenfig Pool and Nature Reserve**
Ton Kenfig
near Pyle
Bridgend CF33 4PT
Tel: 01656 743 386

**Kidwelly Industrial Museum**
Kidwelly
Carmarthenshire SA17 5AD
Tel: 01554 891 078

**Great Orme Copper Mines**
Great Orme
Llandudno
Gwynedd LL30 2XG
Tel: 01492 870 447

**Nanteos Mansion**
Rhydfelin
Aberystwyth
Cardiganshire SY23 4LU
Tel: 01970 624 363

**Merthyr Tydfil Heritage Trust Ltd**
Ynysfach Heritage Centre
Ynysfach Road
Merthyr Tydfil CF48 1AG
Tel: 01685 721 858

**Offa's Dyke Association**
West Street
Knighton
Powys LB7 1EW.
Tel: 01547 528 753

**Penyclawdd Court**
Llanfihangel Crucorney
Abergavenny
Monmouthshire NP7 7LB
Tel: 01873 890 719

**Portmeirion**
Gwynedd LL48 6ET
Tel: 01766 770 228

**Rhondda Heritage Park**
Coedcae Road
Trehafod
Rhondda CF37 7NP
Tel: 01443 682 036

**Tredegar House**
Newport  NP1 9YW
Tel: 01633 815 880

**Welsh Slate Museum (National Museums and Galleries of Wales)**
Gilfach Ddu
Padarn Country Park
Llanberis LL55 4TX
Tel: 01286 871 906

**Wales Tourist Board**
P.O Box 1
Cardiff CF1 2XN
Tel: 01222 475226

# BIBLIOGRAPHY

Barber, Chris, *Mysterious Wales*, Paladin Books, Granada Publishing, St Albans 1982

Beazley, Elizabeth and Brett, Lionel, *Shell Guide to North Wales*, Faber & Faber, London, 1975

Borrow, George, *Wild Wales*, Collins, London & Glasgow, 1969

Bowen, E G, *Saints, Seaways and Settlements*, University of Wales Press, Cardiff 1977

Bowen, E G, *Dewi Sant: St David*, University of Wales Press, Cardiff 1983

Burnham, Helen, *A Guide to Ancient and Historic Wales – Clwyd and Powys*, HMSO, 1995

Cambrensis, Giraldus, *The Itinerary Through Wales*, J M Dent, London, 1908

Davies, John, *A History of Wales*, Penguin Books, London 1994

Davies, Wendy, *Wales in the Early Middle Ages*, Leicester University Press, 1982

Defoe, Daniel, *A Tour Through the Whole Island of Great Britain*, Penguin Books, London, 1971

Dodd, A H, *A Short History of Wales*, B T Batsford. London, 1984

Edwards, G Rhys, (ed), *Snowdonia National Park*, HMSO., 1980

Fenton, Richard, *Tours in Wales 1804–1813*, Cambrian Archaeological Association, London, 1917

Freeman, David, *Guide to Tredegar House*, Newport Borough Council, 1989

Gilpin, William, *Observations on the river Wye*, Woodstock Books, Oxford, 1991

Godwin, Fay and Toulson, Shirley, *The Drovers Roads of Wales*, Wildwood House Ltd, London 1977

Grimes, W F, *The Prehistory of Wales*, National Museum of Wales, Cardiff, 1951

Guest, Charlotte, *The Mabinogion*, Bernard Quaritch, London, 1877

Hadfield, Charles, *Canals of South Wales and The Border*, University of Wales Press, Cardiff, 1960

Hague, Douglas B, *Lighthouses of Wales*, Royal Commission on Ancient and Historical Monuments of Wales, Aberystwyth, 1994

Hilling, J B, *The Historic Architecture of Wales*, University of Wales Press, Cardiff, 1976

Hilling, J B, *Snowdonia and Northern Wales*, B T Batsford, London, 1980

Hilling, J B, *Cardiff and the Valleys*, Lund Humphries, London, 1973

Howell, Peter and Beazley, Elisabeth, *Companion Guide to South Wales*, Collins, London, 1977

Howells, M F, Leveridge, B E and Reedman, A J, *Snowdonia*, Unwin Paperbacks, London, 1981

Hubbard, Edward, *Clwyd (Denbighshire and Flintshire), (The Buildings of Wales series)*, Penguin Books Ltd/University of Wales Press, Harmondsworth, 1986

Jenkins, J Geraint, *The Welsh Woollen Industry*, National Museum of Wales, Cardiff, 1969

John, Brian, *Pembrokeshire*, David & Charles, Newton Abbot, 1976

John, Brian, *The Pembrokeshire Guide*, Greencroft Books, Newport, 1990

Jones, Anthony, *Welsh Chapels*, Alan Sutton Publishing Ltd., and National Museums and Galleries of Wales, Stroud, 1996

Jones, Gareth Elwyn, *Modern Wales: A Concise History*, Cambridge University Press, 1990

Jones, Ieuan Gwynedd, *Observers and Observed: Mid-Victorian Wales*, University of Wales Press, Cardiff, 1992

Jones, J Graham, *The History of Wales, (A Pocket Guide)*, University of Wales Press, Cardiff, 1990

Jones, R Brinley, (ed), *Anatomy of Wales*, Gwerin Publications, Peterston -super – Ely, 1972

Jones, Thomas (ed), *Brut y Tywysogyon (The Chronicle of the Princes)*, University of Wales Press, Cardiff, 1972

Lewis, E D, *The Rhondda Valleys*, University College Press, Cardiff, 1963

Lovegrove, Roger, *The Red Kite*, RSPB, Gomer Press/Kite Country, Llandysul, 1995

Lowe, Jeremy, *Welsh Industrial Workers Housing 1775–1875*, National Museum of Wales, Cardiff, 1985

Malkin, Benjamin Heath, *The Scenery, Antiquities, And Biography of South Wales, Vol I & II*, Longman, Hurst, Rees and Orme, London, 1807

Millward, Roy and Robinson, Adrian, *Landscapes of North Wales*, David & Charles, Newton Abbot, 1978

Musson, Chris, *Wales from the Air: Patterns of Past and Present*, Royal Commission on Ancient and Historical Monuments of Wales, Aberystwyth, and O' Brien, William, *Bronze Age Copper Mining*, Shire Archaeology, Princes Risborough, 1996

Pevsner, Nikolaus and Haslam, Richard, *Powys (The Buildings of Wales series)*, Penguin Books/University of Wales Press, Harmondsworth, 1979

Rees, D Morgan, *The Industrial Archaeology of Wales*, David & Charles, Newton Abbot, 1975

Rowlands, John, *Copper Mountain*, Anglesey Antiquarian Society, Llangefni, 1981

Smith, Bernard and George, T Neville, *British Regional Geology: North Wales*, HMSO, 1987

Smith, Peter, *Houses of the Welsh Countryside*, HMSO, 1975

Sylvester, Dorothy, *A History of Gwynedd*, Phillimore, Chichester, 1983

Thomas, Roger, *Wales, Country Life Books*, Feltham, 1981

Thomas, Roger, *Castles in Wales*, AA/Wales Tourist Board, Basingstoke, 1982

Thomas, Wynford Vaughan and Llewellyn, Alun, *Shell Guide to Wales*, Michael Joseph, London, 1973

Tomes, John (ed), *Blue Guide Wales and The Marches*, Ernest Benn, London & Trowbridge, 1979

Williams, Gwyn A, *When Was Wales*, Penguin Books, London 1985

Williams, Moelwyn, *The South Wales Landscape*, Hodder & Staughton, London, 1975

Whittle, Elisabeth, *The Historic Gardens of Wales*, Cadw/HMSO, 1992

In addition to the publications listed above, much use was made of the guidebooks and information leaflets covering the properties mentioned in the text in the care of Cadw (Welsh Historic Monuments) and the National Trust.

# INDEX

Page numbers in *italics* indicate illustrations